MISSIONAL PREACHING

"*Missional Preaching* should be on every pastor's 'must read' list. It is short and simple, clear and concise, and delightful to read. It will help all of us better engage the multiple cultures and perspectives sitting in our congregations each and every week. I was blessed and challenged by this book. I believe you will be as well."

—**Daniel Akin**, president of Southeastern Baptist Theological Seminary

"The missional frontier comes to our church today, and we must preach not to the choir but to the seekers and critics, adversaries and mockers. Stephen Stallard's book is helpful in this process of becoming more missional in our preaching. It resonates with my own experience and challenges me to preach more confidently and experiment more creatively. Being born and raised in a Christian home in the former USSR meant staying isolated from the hostile Soviet society to survive and protect ourselves. Yet, my parents and grandparents found enough opportunities to preach on the frontier of unbelief and hostility, even in trials, even in prison. They once lived and preached on the missional frontier, and they served well. How about us today? How about our churches? Please, read the book and answer the questions."

—**Rev. Dr. Michael Cherenkov**, senior pastor, Revival Baptist Church, Vancouver, WA

"In his book, *Missional Preaching: Communicating the Gospel in an Age of Unbelief*, Stephen Stallard has provided a wonderful resource for preachers and teachers everywhere. There is no shortage of books on preaching, and perhaps the only thing rivaling the advance of secularity in our age is the proliferation of books about secularity in our age. Nevertheless, this book is a fresh contribution of valuable insight that is both theologically grounded in the good news of Christ and immensely practical, filled with timely principles for today. You will benefit greatly from reading this!"

—**Josh Matthews**, PhD, dean, Western Seminary

"Stephen Stallard is the ideal person to write about missional preaching in North America. First, he has served as a pastor on both coasts—in Brooklyn, New York, and now in Portland, Oregon. Second, Stephen is a terrific writer who knows how to turn a phrase. His writing is delightful to read. Third, this book is rich in both biblical and historical reflection. It is practical, as well. It has helped me. I already plan on rereading it and recommending it to my preaching students and my pastor friends."

—**Steven D. Matthewson**, adjunct professor in preaching and biblical studies, Western Seminary

"Stephen Stallard brings the knowledge and the experience needed for us to think through how to preach the old, old story in an age of tumult. This book guides us through crafting and communicating the message while knowing which words are dulled by cultural familiarity and which are obscured by cultural confusion. Preachers and teachers will be glad to learn from this solid, thoughtful guide."

—**Russell Moore**, editor in chief, *Christianity Today*

"This is a winsome wake-up call for all preachers in our late modern context. Whether we like it or not, we must come to terms with the fact that God has placed us on a missional frontier. Drawing from both Scripture and the testimony of Christian history, Stephen offers an engaging and reliable guide in calling for contextual, commonsense, confessional, caring, and Christ-centered *missional preaching*. I definitely recommend this read."

—**Dan Strange**, director, Crosslands Forum

Stephen Stallard

MISSIONAL PREACHING

Communicating the Gospel in an Age of Unbelief

B&H
ACADEMIC®
BRENTWOOD, TENNESSEE

Published by B&H Academic®
Brentwood, Tennessee

ISBN: 978-1-4300-9402-9

Dewey Decimal Classification: 251
Subject Heading: PREACHING \ PASTORAL THEOLOGY \ SERMONS

Cover design by Kristen Ingebretson.
Cover images from Shutterstock.

Printed in the United States of America

30 29 28 27 26 25 VP 1 2 3 4 5 6 7 8 9 10

To Malia Adele

CONTENTS

INTRODUCTION: PREACHING PAST THE CHOIR

When I was a kid, church life revolved, in part, around the choir. That included choir practices, Christmas pageants, adult choirs, youth choirs, kids' choirs, and revival choirs. The choir was essential to church culture (at least where I'm from, in the American South). It was to the church what apple pie is to America. And yet, of all the churches I've ministered in as an adult, none of them consistently used a traditional choir. Many evangelical churches have shifted their approach, using more contemporary methods, like praise bands. In many churches, the choir has vanished.

Now, this isn't a diatribe about worship methods. I, for one, have been happy to pastor churches that are committed to engaging modern people with styles that are both rooted in the gospel and connected to the music of today. But the missing choir is emblematic of a larger point.

In the past, pastors could "preach to the choir." They could assume they had a base of support: Christians who were probably mature in their faith. Preachers could preach, knowing that the choir would back them up (literally and metaphorically). They could preach about the evils "out there" in the culture and count on a knowing chorus of "amens" from the choir. They could explain the blasphemous beliefs of false religions, knowing their listeners (especially the choir) would be horrified by those profane views. They also knew that no one would disagree with the preacher, partly because there were no representatives of those other faiths in the room.

In the twenty-first century, the choir has all but disappeared, and not just literally. Many worship leaders have adapted their styles, replacing choirs with bands. But an even bigger shift is underway. Preachers can no longer preach on Sundays and assume that their listeners share their religious sensibilities. The choir is gone, and it's not coming back.

Now, when we stand behind our pulpits (or music stands), we see a different set of listeners. Those who hear our sermons are people who have been molded by an era characterized by secularism, deconstruction, and pluralism. How does this affect their ability to hear our sermons? And how do we get through to them?

A Secular Age

In America (and in the West, more broadly) we are living in a secular age. Canadian philosopher Charles Taylor has explored the intellectual roots of this society and how we got here.[1] He argues that society has gone on a journey, one that took the West from the Reformation era (in which belief was typical) to the late-modern era (in which skepticism is increasingly typical). Few would challenge Taylor's notion that we live in a secular age. But what does that mean, and how does it affect those of us preaching today? I believe that four traits of our secular age directly affect our preaching, whether we like it or not.

First, in our secular age unbelief is plausible. Of course, there have always been atheists and agnostics. Ever since the fall, people have expressed their disbelief toward their Creator. In previous times, however, unbelief felt more tenuous. It is not that unbelief was impossible. It is just that it was socially implausible. For instance, medieval European villages were built around the local church. It was the most important structure in the town, and the priest (as resident expert on many topics) presided over the hub of community life.

As a modern urban dweller, I have no desire to return to ancient villages that lack the modern amenities of city life. And as someone formed by the Baptist tradition, I have no desire to return to a paradigm that forces me to conform my religious beliefs and practices to fit in with the rest of society. Still, I am keenly aware that a seismic shift has occurred. Previously, society was structured in such a way that people believed (at least on paper) and fell in step with societal religious norms. Few dared

[1] See Charles Taylor, *A Secular Age* (Belknap, 2007).

to cling to rival religions because the social costs were too high. Belief was a given, and unbelief was implausible.

Today, the tides of secularism have come in, and unbelief is commonplace. Indeed, it is celebrated. From Main Street to the metaverse, people proudly fly the flag of disbelief. In our era we cannot take for granted that people find it easy to believe. In fact, many of our neighbors might think that doubt is the intellectually responsible choice. How do we get through to them?

Second, in our secular age, disenchantment is normal. The woods used to be haunted by angels and demons, monsters and dragons, witches and wizards. The medieval world was inundated with the supernatural. Hardly anyone doubted the existence of an unseen realm. Drought? Caused by demons who were angry at you. Famine? The result of an angelic war. Plague? God was judging you. Medieval people had these automatic impulses in response to the world around them. They believed the universe was enchanted.

Those who lived in medieval times were at the mercy of the spiritual world. That is why they prayed and came to church. They desperately needed God to smile on their farmland, to bless their trade, to enable their survival in a world full of chaos.

Fast-forward to the twenty-first century. People in the West no longer live like that. We have developed modern systems of irrigation to help our crops flourish. We have taken out insurance, so we are cared for in case of disaster. The government can step in to meet most of our needs. God is no longer necessary because all of our big problems have apparently been solved. Natural problems demand natural solutions. God, as a supernatural being, seems unnecessary in the modern world.

We are preaching to people who have become disenchanted. Many are trapped in what Taylor calls the "immanent frame."[2] They are unable to conceive of a spiritual realm outside their own. When we step into the pulpit and expound texts that refer to demons and angels, to heaven and hell, we elicit immediate disbelief from some. Worse still, when we mention that all-important true story of the pregnant virgin, we are greeted with at least some measure of incredulity. In a universe that is disenchanted, the virgin birth seems unserious. And yet, we preach before people who are shaped by the disenchanting forces of our age. How do we get through to them?

Third, in our secular age, spirituality is remixed. That's how journalist Tara Isabella Burton describes the present cultural moment. In her book *Strange Rites: New Religions for a Godless World,* she points out that secularism is on the rise, but so are strange new spiritual mash-ups. People who identify as having no religious beliefs (famously called the "nones") often engage in deeply spiritual practices, sampled from a variety of religious expressions.[3]

Having done pastoral ministry in eclectic cultural contexts (from Jamaican to Chinese), my palate has become global. I enjoy eating food from around the world. What's more, I appreciate well-done fusion dishes, which combine cuisines from multiple cultures, like the Korean taco I bought at a food truck

---

[2] See Taylor, chap. 15, "The Immanent Frame" (539–93).

[3] Tara Isabella Burton, *Strange Rites: New Religions for a Godless World* (Public Affairs, 2020).

in Austin or the sushi burrito I devoured at a Manhattan food court. This is fusion food at its finest: bringing the best of two cuisines together to create something fresh. But that doesn't happen only with food.

In the twenty-first century, it seems somehow chic to mix rituals from astrology with practices from Christianity and ancient Druidism. In a hyper-connected digital era, access to spirituality is virtually unlimited. People can now mix and remix their religious ideologies and practices as fast as their broadband will permit. Do you want to be a Jedi who dabbles in Islam? Cool. There's a space for you in a secular age. When we preach, we are engaging people who feel liberated to choose their spirituality in the same way they select food at a buffet.

Fourth and finally, in our secular age, distraction is rampant. Our phones have changed us. A generation that lives in the perpetual glow of a tiny screen inevitably forgets how to engage with truths presented in a sermon. In the digital world, if you get bored, you keep scrolling or you open a streaming app. One-minute TikTok videos and filtered Instagram stories have reshaped what types of content we want to engage with, and for how long.

Preachers stand behind the sacred desk and open something incredibly old-fashioned—a book. It's a book we claim is ancient, yet relevant. It's a book we cherish, but one that our listeners might not have time for. This does not mean that sermons should be delivered with the panache or pace of social media. Rather, it means that we are going to have to figure out how to break through the attention deficit. Our listeners are distracted. How do we get through to them?

A Deconstructing Age

We don't simply preach in a secular moment; we preach in the age of deconstruction. A decade ago, deconstruction was a topic for philosophy classes. Now deconstruction has gone mainstream. Everywhere we look, Christians are deconstructing their faith. Sometimes this manifests itself more modestly, as faithful followers of Jesus seek to strip away the cultural baggage that has been added to the faith. This is a good pursuit, and necessary in every generation if the goal is to faithfully reconstruct according to Scripture.

Much of the time, however, deconstruction is the dismantling of the historic faith that was delivered to the saints (Jude 3). Members of our churches are rethinking marriage and sexuality. They are shifting their views on hell. They are uncertain about the deity of Christ.[4] Some of this is due to poor teaching. We must do a better job of transmitting the faith to the next generation. Some of this may also be tied to the tarnished reputation of American evangelicalism. Through scandal, hypocrisy, and unwise political engagement, the church has lost the trust of a rising generation of Americans. We must do a better job living out the faith that was passed down to us.

Jim Davis and Michael Graham provide staggering statistical context for the phenomenon of deconstruction: "We're currently living in the largest and fastest religious shift in US history. Some 40 million adult Americans who used to go to church

[4] The State of Theology (an outreach of Ligonier), 2022, https://thestateoftheology.com/.

at least once per month now attend less than once per year. This shift is larger than the number of conversions during the First Great Awakening, Second Great Awakening, and the totality of the Billy Graham Crusades combined."[5] Not all dechurched people have deconstructed the Christian faith. Countless people who are dechurched still believe and might return to church. However, many appear to have walked away forever.

The accelerating trend of deconstruction seems, in part, to be fueled by societal peer pressure. It is no longer acceptable to embrace the ethic of Jesus. Perhaps it never was. Younger evangelicals are wary of being canceled and nervous of being on the wrong side of history. So they shade the truth, shifting here and there, until—without intending to—they have abandoned Christianity. This will usually show up first in the youth ministry. The youth pastor is often the first one to field questions from teens who are grappling with their doubts and wondering about the truth of Christianity and the goodness of God. A team of researchers cited the example of Steve Jobs, who was not satisfied by the answers his pastor gave him and departed from the faith. They note, "Young people like Steve who swim in the deep end of challenging cultural and developmental questions often view the church as merely splashing around in the shallow end."[6] We

---

[5] Jim Davis and Michael Graham, "5 Misconceptions about Dechurching in America," Gospel Coalition, September 5, 2023, https://www.thegospelcoalition.org/article/misconceptions-dechurching/.

[6] Kara Powell, Jake Mulder, and Brad Griffin, *Growing Young: 6 Essential Strategies to Help Young People Discover and Love Your Church* (Baker, 2016), 90.

must do a better job of discipling these would-be deconstructors in our midst. And that, in many ways, begins with preaching.

For a variety of reasons, some (perhaps many) of the members of our churches are on the verge of deconstructing. We may not know it yet, but they harbor deep doubts about the Bible, about God, about human sexuality. How do we preach to those who are about to deconstruct or have already started deconstructing?

A Pluralistic Age

For many Americans, "missions" is something we used to do somewhere else. Now, due to a variety of factors, missions work flows in all directions. It takes place both globally and in our neighborhoods. In America, globalization, immigration, and the internet have sparked an increase in the number of practitioners of non-Christian religions. Buddhism is popular, especially in its Westernized, Zen form. The rituals of Hinduism are on the rise, and meditation apps are trending. Various streams of Islam are advancing, thanks to high birth rates and outreach among the incarcerated.

If a local church is evangelistic, members of other faiths will be engaged with the gospel. That means that they will, at least occasionally, be present at worship services because a friend invited them. When I was a church planter in New York City, I preached regularly to members of other faiths. During one of our open-air services in the neighborhood park, Hasidic Jews walked nearby during my sermon. Afterward, a young girl with a Muslim head covering played with the kids of our church.

It was not just our outdoor services. From time to time, I preached to members of other faiths who identified as Rastafarian, Buddhist, Muslim, Odinist, and even as practitioners of the Nation of Islam. This didn't happen each Sunday, but I had to be ready in case they came. I prepared my sermons with these folks in mind. In a church plant, evangelistic engagement is the goal. You start a church in the hopes that God will draw unbelievers to him. Even in an established church, this still happens more than we might realize.

Sometimes our neighbors are there because we were friendly, and our coworkers are there because of a special event hosted by the church. Many of them struggle to sit through the sermons at our churches precisely because they do not believe. They identify as members of another faith or none at all. How do we show respect for their religious beliefs without agreeing with them? How do we acknowledge their presence and still preach the Name that is above every other name (Phil 2:9)?

You may think that this type of missional preaching encounter is too foreign to your own ministry context. To that, I would say: not for long. Secularism, deconstruction, and pluralism are spreading across the country, affecting denominations, churches, and cities. Your city, wherever it is, will soon be affected by these forces, and it could end up resembling places like New York and Portland, Oregon, where I'm currently pastoring. Indeed, the numbers of those who identify as nonreligious (the nones) are growing rapidly throughout the United States. Stephen Bullivant notes, "Having no religion is no longer the preserve of nonconformists or self-consciously quirky enclaves like Portland or Austin. . . . With each passing year, being a none is rapidly becoming less socially and culturally odd." He continues, "In many places, among many groups, nonreligiosity is now thoroughly normal. It is now a perfectly established and respectable 'live' option for most people. That's not true of everywhere, of course. Yet like other erstwhile Portland specialties as craft beer, artisanal donuts, and veganism, it's gone mainstream."[7]

Portland is determined to, as the locals say, keep it weird. And Portland is coming to a city near you. With a new missional frontier on your doorstep, it makes sense to prepare to preach to those being shaped by the ideas of secularism, deconstruction, and pluralism.

Plotting a Course for Preaching in a Post-Christian Age

The rest of this book will be an exploration of missional preaching. It is a book written for you who preach on the missional frontier, whether as a youth pastor, teaching pastor, or church planter. It is designed to help you plot a course for preaching in our new, bewildering, post-Christian age. Although plenty of theory undergirds this book, this is not a theoretical volume. It is for practitioners, by someone who has spent more than a decade preaching on the missional frontier, first on the East Coast (Brooklyn) and then the West Coast (Portland). As we plot a

[7] Stephen Bullivant, *Nonverts: The Making of Ex-Christian America* (Oxford, 2022), 72–73.

course for preaching in this new era, we will discover six crucial tips for missional preaching:

1. Watch your tone.
2. Acknowledge the elephant in the room.
3. Narrate the true story of the world.
4. Be ready to answer.
5. Celebrate truth, goodness, and beauty.
6. Preach Jesus.

In each chapter, we will explore each strategy through three lenses: Scripture, history, and method. We will see how preachers in the Bible adopted these strategies (Scripture), how preachers throughout history have adopted these strategies (history), and how to put these strategies into action (method).

As we embark upon this journey, here is my basic definition of missional preaching: *missional preaching engages people at the frontier of unbelief and invites them to take a journey toward Jesus.* My prayer for this book is that it might motivate you to preach boldly on that missional frontier. As you do, you will discover that the choir has vanished. But that will not intimidate you, because Jesus stands with you, on the frontier, as you preach. Through his power, we must do more than preach to the choir.

1

Watch Your Tone

There they are: I see them every Sunday. As a pastor at a church in suburban Portland, I have the privilege of preaching to a couple on a faith journey. I first spoke to the wife, who told me that she didn't yet call herself a Christian. She was still trying to sort out her beliefs. Her husband, she said, was once a member of another religious tribe. Now they both attend our church every week, exploring the claims of Christ. From the pulpit, I can see them processing my sermons in real time.

Every sermon I preach is filtered through the prism of this couple's spiritual search and our emerging relationship with them. When I preach about the truth of the Bible, I recognize that they are not yet fully convinced. Knowing about their journey forces me to watch my tone.

Watch your tone! It's a command, or a rebuke, given by someone who feels disrespected by someone else. We want to be respected. I have had many conversations in which I was told I was wrong, sometimes by a church member, a coworker, a teacher, or my wife and kids. Usually, I am more receptive to critique when it is delivered gently. When someone raises his or her voice in anger, something inside me responds in kind. My pride rears its head, and I stubbornly resist the critique, even if it is right on target.

That same dynamic is at play in preaching. People are prone to resist the truth because they are sinners. But our pride raises the stakes and prompts us to resist conviction when we feel disrespected. Missional preachers understand human nature and preach accordingly.

This does not mean watering down the truth of the gospel. Paul was a preeminent preacher of the gospel, and he acknowledged that the gospel is offensive (Gal 5:11). The idea that we are sinners in need of outside rescue is offensive to human pride. Some will react in anger to such a message. So be it. We cannot alter the gospel. But let us make sure that it is the gospel that offends, not our careless speech.

The gospel is a stumbling block to the Jews and foolishness to the Greeks (1 Cor 1:23). People will stumble over the message of the cross. I hope they do not stumble because of my thoughtless sermon. People might deem the gospel foolish. Hopefully, they do not turn away from Jesus because I act foolishly, whether in the pulpit or outside of it. This dichotomy is what Peter referred to when he said that people ought to criticize us because they reject our God, rather than because we are behaving ungodly (1 Peter 2–3).

I grew up in a Christian family, and I am still haunted by a joke I shared about Mormonism. First, some background: Mormons believe that the angel Moroni, guardian of secret, buried plates, appeared to Joseph Smith and that the revelations he granted to Smith undergird the Book of Mormon. To Mormons, the angel symbolizes restoration. Moroni is so significant in the history of Mormonism that a Moroni statue tops many Mormon temples.[1]

As an orthodox Christian, I cannot accept the teachings of Mormonism. Although Mormons claim to be followers of Jesus, Mormon beliefs and practices mark them as outside of authentic Christian faith. In my estimation, they are a people to be evangelized. We should preach the gospel to Mormons.

Now, back to the joke. I did not start it, but I participated in it by laughing and repeating the joke. We would refer to Moroni as the Angel Macaroni. The joke elicited laughs and eye rolls every time. But that response stood for something else. With our laughter, we indicated that Mormonism was something to laugh about. *How could Mormons believe in something so bizarre?* we thought. Rather than engage their unorthodox ideas, we laughed at them. Rather than unmask their idolatry, we told jokes at their expense.

Imagine a Mormon overhearing such a lighthearted conversation. Imagine she has worked up the courage to attend the

---

[1] The Church of Jesus Christ of Latter-day Saints, "Angel Moroni," churchofjesuschrist.org, accessed August 27, 2024, https://www.churchofjesuschrist.org/study/history/topics/angel-moroni?lang=eng.

evangelical church of her friend, who has persistently invited her. And on her first visit, she hears the preacher crack a joke about her tribe. He does not take her seriously. Instead, she feels dismissed. It will be her last visit to that evangelical church. She returns to the Mormon temple, vowing never to go back to an evangelical church. And she never does. Watching our tone is a matter of life and death.

When I preach to those whose journey has not yet led them across the threshold of faith, I understand that they are faced with a choice. Every sermon, they are introduced to Jesus. Every sermon, they face a decision to accept him or reject him. I want to ensure that my non-Christian listeners do not feel belittled or pressured into accepting Christ. That is not the way of Jesus. Instead, I want them to behold the glory of Christ as the Word is proclaimed in the sermon.

If watching your tone is not watering down the gospel, what is it? Quite simply, it is the Golden Rule of Preaching. It is preaching to others the way you want to be preached to. Watching your tone is preaching with honesty, humility, and love (we will return to these ideas in a later section). Before we explore practical tips to help us with our tone, it is fair to ask if anyone has ever tried this before. I believe the answer is yes.

Daniel

It is difficult to imagine a more hostile context than the ancient city of Babylon. Yet it was here that Daniel, first as an underage slave, and then later as a royal adviser, honed his witness. Daniel was no ordinary prophet. As a young man, he was ripped from the safe confines of his home in Jerusalem. He was deported to Babylon, where he was immersed in an alien cultural setting. He was forced to undergo a rigorous cultural reeducation curriculum. In an insult to both his culture and his religion, he was forced to swap out his Jewish name for a Babylonian name.[2] The name Daniel (which means "God is judge") was retired, and in its place the prophet was called Belteshazzar, which some scholars translate "Bel, protect the King."[3] Since Bel was one of the false gods of Babylon, every time Daniel's new name was uttered, he was reminded of his location on the missional frontier.

From his vantage point in Babylon, Daniel could not hear the all-important Shema uttered aloud ("Listen, Israel: The LORD our God, the LORD is one," Deut 6:4). He could not smell the incense offered up by the priests in the Jewish temple. He could not taste the bitter herbs of the Passover meal that reminded Jews of their liberation from slavery. He could not see the beautiful temple that served as a reminder of the presence of God among his people. Instead, he heard prayers offered in a strange language to foreign gods. He smelled the aroma of meat that had probably been offered to idols. He tasted the bitter sting of life as a slave in exile. And he watched in horror as holy vessels belonging to Yahweh were housed in the temple of an impostor (Dan 1:2).

---

[2] Christopher J. H. Wright, *Hearing the Message of Daniel: Sustaining Faith in Today's World* (Zondervan, 2017), 27–34.

[3] Ernest C. Lucas, *Daniel*, Apollos Old Testament Commentary (Apollos, 2002), 53.

This life of exile could have jaded Daniel. He could have become cynical and adopted a harsh posture toward his captors. He could have rained withering, angry critiques down upon the leaders of Babylon. Instead, Daniel watched his tone.

The prophet interacted with at least three kings: Nebuchadnezzar, Belshazzar, and Darius. He never sugarcoated his message. Although he worked for these pagan kings, he understood his vocation as the servant of Yahweh. He spoke on God's behalf to the Babylonian and Persian kings who enslaved and employed him. He spoke truth to power. Yet somehow Daniel managed to maintain a good relationship with two of these kings, even as he uttered unpopular words from God. His interactions with the Babylonian king Nebuchadnezzar and the Persian king Darius demonstrate that he, at the very least, knew how to speak to them with kindness. Our tone matters.

Daniel probably had the most reason to be bitter at Nebuchadnezzar. After all, it was Nebuchadnezzar who had besieged Jerusalem, ransacked the temple, and enslaved Daniel and his peers. If I had been a slave in Babylon, I would have seethed in rage. There would have been no hiding it. It would come out in my speech as I interacted with the powerful rulers of Babylon.

But this was not Daniel's path. Recognizing God's sovereignty over his situation, he chose the way of peace without compromise. In the book of Daniel, the Hebrew slave interacts with Nebuchadnezzar twice. The first time, he interprets a dream about a colossal statue, and in the process, he saves the lives of the Babylonian magicians (Daniel 2). The second time, he interprets an ominous dream about Nebuchadnezzar's destiny (Daniel 4).

When Daniel first stood before the king, he had every reason to be afraid. Here he was, a Hebrew in a strange land, standing before one who had been his enemy. He was standing before a ruler who could order his execution without remorse. Daniel's life was at stake, and he knew it. Nebuchadnezzar had threatened to kill off an entire class of people: the Babylonian wise men (magicians, mediums, sorcerers, and Chaldeans). He was upset because they could not interpret his dream. They protested, of course. *How can we interpret your dream if you do not first tell us what was in the dream?*

Why did Nebuchadnezzar not want to reveal his dream? Perhaps he suspected that his sorcerers would make something up to save their lives. The king wanted honesty. He wanted answers. If his wise men were really in touch with the Divine, he reasoned they could discern both his dream and its interpretation. When his magicians stumbled, the king pounced. In a fit of rage, he issued a fateful decree: All the wise men of Babylon (including Daniel and his Hebrew friends) would be executed.

"Daniel responded with tact and discretion" by approaching Arioch, the captain of the king's guard (Dan 2:14). He asked him what was up: *Why are you preparing to execute us?* Once Daniel perceived the problem, he went to the king to buy some time. For reasons unknown, Nebuchadnezzar seems to have said yes. Instead of executing his sorcerers, he waited on Daniel. Meanwhile, Daniel asked his friends to pray while he waited on God.

When God revealed the mystery in a nighttime vision, Daniel first worshipped the King of heaven and then quickly returned to the court of the king of Babylon. There, with his life on the line, he interpreted the dream. What is interesting is not the meaning of the giant statue (I will leave that to Old Testament scholars and theologians). What is crucial for this book is *how* Daniel talked to the king. Three times Daniel addressed Nebuchadnezzar according to protocol: "Your Majesty." After three years of training, the Hebrew slave knew how to address a Babylonian king.

Even more noteworthy is how Daniel described Nebuchadnezzar. He said, "Your Majesty, you are king of kings. The God of the heavens has given you sovereignty, power, strength, and glory" (Dan 2:37). Some might view this as flattery: Daniel knew his life hung in the balance, so he complimented the king. However, I think it was more than that. Daniel was politely and respectfully employing the protocols of the royal court to present a word from the Lord. He was speaking for God, which is something preachers dare to do every Sunday.

Daniel was polite and formal in how he addressed the most powerful man on the planet. But he did not water down his message. He made it clear who is the real boss: Yahweh! Nebuchadnezzar was only powerful because God had allowed him to be. Daniel knew how to wed theology with mission. He respectfully spoke truth to power. The prophet knew how to watch his tone.

Some might suspect that this was a one-off event. Daniel's tone was only kind because his life hung in the balance. But as we see in their next encounter, Daniel and Nebuchadnezzar seem to have developed a relationship of sorts. I am not saying that they became friends (would you befriend a bloodthirsty despot?), but at least they were not enemies. The next time Daniel interpreted the king's dream, he had attained the rank of chief magician (Dan 4:9). His promotion was both a sign of God's favor and of the king's respect.

Nebuchadnezzar told his favorite wise man his unnerving dream: a large, beautiful tree was situated in the middle of the earth. A watcher then appeared to pronounce judgment on the tree. It was to be chopped down, and it would become like a beast for seven periods of time.

Daniel knew right away that this dream was about his boss. His initial response is worth quoting in full: "Then Daniel, whose name is Belteshazzar, was stunned for a moment, and his thoughts alarmed him. The king said, 'Belteshazzar, don't let the dream or its interpretation alarm you.' Belteshazzar answered, 'My lord, may the dream apply to those who hate you, and its interpretation to your enemies!'" (Dan 4:19). Daniel did not have to say any of those words. Yet, stunned by the dream, he responded with empathy. It seems that Daniel had developed some sort of care and concern for the tyrant. His gracious tone emerged from a compassionate heart.

However, Daniel's empathy did not lead him to water down the message. He was unflinching in his interpretation: God had decreed that the proud Nebuchadnezzar would become like an animal. For a time, he would lose his perch atop the world as he battled temporary insanity. Daniel pleaded with the king:

"Therefore, may my advice seem good to you my king. Separate yourself from your sins by doing what is right, and from your injustices by showing mercy to the needy. Perhaps there will be an extension of your prosperity" (Dan 4:27). Daniel cared about Nebuchadnezzar, so he spoke to him winsomely and tenderly, pleading for his soul. He knew how to watch his tone. This is missional preaching.

One more vignette demonstrates that Daniel honed this technique on the missional frontier. After the rise of the Persian Empire, Daniel became a key administrator in the regime of King Darius. Motivated by jealousy, Daniel's Persian peers crafted legislation banning prayer to anyone but Darius. They knew that Daniel was a devout Jew and that he would pray only to Yahweh as God.

Caught in their trap, Daniel immediately experienced the empathy of the king. Darius "made every effort until sundown to deliver him" (Dan 6:14). When he could not, he cast Daniel into the lions' den and prayed for a miracle. After a sleepless night, Darius returned to the mouth of the cave and asked if Daniel was alive. Notice the prophet's response: "May the king live forever. My God sent his angel and shut the lions' mouths; and they haven't harmed me, for I was found innocent before him. And also before you, Your Majesty, I have not done harm" (Dan 6:21–22).

Once again, we hear notes of respect and care. Daniel uses words of protocol ("May the king live forever" and "Your Majesty") and he stresses that he has not sinned against the king. By now, Daniel was a veteran of these interreligious interactions, having spent a lifetime on the missional frontier. He never compromised the truth of his beliefs. He was willing to stick his neck out and be punished for his faith. But he had also learned to watch his tone.

Missional preaching is not watering down our message to make it more appealing to outsiders. Instead, it is crafting a winsome tone that is nourished by an empathetic imagination. When we preach on the frontier of unbelief, we must remember that we are not pioneers. A Hebrew prophet has preceded us and showed us that, although it is costly, there is a biblically faithful and missionally sensitive way to preach in Babylon.

Billy Graham

"America's Preacher." That's what *Time* magazine called Billy Graham in its commemorative issue, published just after his death.[4] They were right. Rarely has a preacher been so embraced and revered by so much of society. Graham preached to millions, in mass crusades from Los Angeles to New York City and around the world. His sermons were broadcast on television, multiplying his gospel witness. In fact, my own book probably wouldn't exist apart from the ministry of Billy Graham.

My father and his twin brother grew up in a moral but non-Christian family. They did not attend church, but they did watch Graham's sermons on TV. Graham usually ended his sermons

---

[4] "Billy Graham: America's Preacher," *Time Commemorative Edition,* 2018.

by exhorting his viewers to find a nearby church to attend. My father and my uncle were so moved by the preaching of the renowned evangelist that they purposed to find a church in which the preaching sounded "like Billy Graham." Eventually, at age twenty, they found one, and trusted Christ after several months of listening to the sermons. Without Graham's missional influence, my father never would have married my mother (a member of the choir at the church he sought out). I would have never been born. And you would not be reading this. God's providence is mysteriously wonderful.

Graham had a compelling way of communicating to the heart. He could speak directly to the skeptics in his audience: "Oh, on the outside you put on a big front. You laugh and you joke and all the rest, but when you're alone, there it is—that void, that aching, that empty place. There is a questing; there is a hunger; there is a longing for something else in life; and you haven't found it yet and you want it."[5] It was those insightful appeals to the heart that the Holy Spirit used to draw my father and my uncle to Christ.

In addition to his televised sermons and mass crusades, Graham, like the prophet Daniel, was an adviser to world leaders. He functioned as an unofficial chaplain to presidents, and he personally knew every American president from Truman to Obama. He earned their trust by promising never to divulge what they shared in confidence. Even presidents need a pastor, and Graham was able to hear their confidential confessions and

[5] "Billy Graham," *Time*, 54.

offer the hope of the gospel to them. He mourned with them when they buried their loved ones. He answered their questions about God. He challenged them privately to acknowledge their sin and turn to Christ. Graham learned to watch his tone as he provided pastoral care to the most powerful men in the world.[6]

Due to this trust and to Graham's stature as "America's Pastor," the nation turned to the ailing Graham in the aftermath of the 9/11 terrorist attacks. Reeling from a horrifying attack on New York and Washington, the nation searched for a moment of spiritual catharsis. President George W. Bush invited his religious mentor (the one who had famously led him to Christ) to offer a reflection in the Washington National Cathedral.

Three thousand were dead, and with America's anger and heartache abounding, the elderly evangelist ascended to the pulpit and addressed a fearful, hurting nation. He acknowledged that many of his listeners might be wondering why God allowed the evil attacks to happen. In empathetic, pastoral tones, he even assured those who were angry at God that the Creator understands their feelings. He then pivoted and declared, "But God can be trusted, even when life seems at its darkest."[7]

Graham's tender tone invited Americans of all religious backgrounds to ponder the meaning of life in this dark hour. In an ecumenical service, it might be expected that Graham would

---

[6] Nancy Gibbs and Michael Duffy, *The Preacher and the Presidents: Billy Graham in the White House* (Center Street, 2007).

[7] "Billy Graham's 9/11[/01] Message from the Washington National Cathedral," YouTube, 11:28, Billy Graham Evangelistic Association, https://www.youtube.com/watch?v=VptxoWl0pxI.

water down the gospel message to speak with broader appeal. But that was not the route chosen by the distinguished missional preacher. He opted to proclaim Christ and Christ crucified: "The cross tells us that God understands our sin, and our suffering, for he took upon himself in the person of Jesus Christ our sins and our suffering. And from the cross, God declares 'I love you. I know the heartaches and the sorrows and the pains you feel. But I love you.'"[8]

Graham is an example of a preacher who learned to watch his tone. He could speak to distraught Americans at a fragile moment, ministering to them with a gentle tone and compassionate words. Yet his tone did not detract from his message. He preached the gospel to a watching world.

The example of Billy Graham also showcases what can happen when we do compromise our witness to gain (or keep) an unbelieving audience. Unlike many of his contemporaries, Graham lived a largely scandal-free life. But there was one exception. When the Watergate tapes were released, Graham's close friendship with disgraced President Richard Nixon was thrown into a new light.

Graham had steadfastly defended Nixon, declaring him to be a man of integrity. He used his influence to assure Americans that the president was a moral man. Tragically, the closeness of his relationship clouded his judgment, blinding him to the truth. Eventually, the Oval Office tapes were released, and the world

---

[8] "Billy Graham's 9/11 Message from the Washington National Cathedral."

knew the darkness that enveloped the White House. Graham was shocked. In his autobiography, Graham recalled, "On the day the contents of the White House tapes were made public and I heard the President's words, I was deeply distressed. The thing that surprised and shook me most was the vulgar language he used. . . . Inwardly, I felt torn apart."[9]

Things got worse many years later when a tape was released proving that Nixon and Graham had engaged in anti-Semitic banter following a 1972 prayer breakfast. Billy Graham was crushed by the evidence of his sin, which he said he could not remember. He candidly acknowledged that he was wrong and begged for forgiveness.[10] I believe that Billy Graham understandably wanted to maintain his ability to preach to President Nixon. And so, without realizing it, he compromised his witness to maintain his audience. Most preachers have felt that temptation. Some of us have given in to it.

Like Daniel in Babylon, Graham preached to the powerful. Like the Hebrew prophet, he learned to watch his tone, choosing respect and empathy over vitriol and ridicule. Unlike Daniel, he was swept up in the sinful currents of culture, compromising his gospel witness in his association with Richard Nixon.

As we preach on the missional frontier, we should learn from both Graham's successes and his failures. We should strive to present a clear gospel message, as the evangelist did after 9/11. We should imitate his style, opting for kindness over combativeness.

---

[9] Billy Graham, *Just as I Am* (Harper Collins, 1997), 457.

[10] "Billy Graham," *Time*, 93.

But we should also be wary of the danger of forgetting whom we serve. In every era, people long to be told what they want to hear. Missional preachers engage people with kindness and sensitivity, but they never change the content of the gospel. They are not ashamed of the gospel, because it is the power of God unto salvation (see Rom 1:16).

The Golden Rule of Preaching

Nothing I have said about tone is revolutionary. In fact, it is quite basic. It is the Golden Rule of Preaching: In your sermons, treat others the way you want to be treated. But in a polarized society, in which conflict is the norm, watching our tone is a countercultural practice. Our neighbors can tune in to their preferred cable news channel to witness rhetorical combat, delivered nightly by their favorite pundits. When they come to church, things should be different. It is not just that what we say is different, but how we say it is distinct as well. Our message is unique, and our method should be strangely peaceful in an angry world. The Golden Rule of Preaching means embracing the Christian virtues of honesty, humility, and love. If the tone of our sermons is shaped by these virtues, we will be in a better position to preach on the emerging missional frontier.

Honesty—of course my sermons are characterized by honesty! At least, I think they are. As Christians, we know that God cannot lie, and that he calls us to be people of the truth (Titus 1:2). Telling the truth is important to the God who is Truth (John 14:6). In fact, bearing false witness made the short list in the Old Testament. Ten rules summarized the entire biblical law. One of them was a command to tell the truth about our neighbors (Exod 20:16).

Too often, preachers fail to follow this admonition. We shade the truth, a little here, a little there. We want to make the illustration a bit richer, the argument a little stronger. Every preacher has faced the temptation to skirt the truth in the pulpit. Some of us have faced the temptation to create a straw man when we are talking about those who are outside the faith. It is easy to say that atheists, Muslims, or Jehovah's Witnesses believe this or that. People in our congregations might nod along, maybe even say "Amen." Some, however, may whip out their smartphones to fact-check the sermon in real time. And when that happens, what's next?

What happens to our witness when we paint the other side in a falsely negative light? What happens to our sermons when our unbelieving listeners recognize that we are not being entirely honest? We will fail to reach those on the missional frontier if we sacrifice honesty in our sermons. We must resist the urge to caricature people on the other side. We must not demolish straw-man arguments that leaders on the other side would never make.

This takes work. It requires diligence. If striving for total honesty makes a sermon a little less polished, then so be it. Earlier in the chapter, I referenced my own missteps referencing the Angel Moroni. You may have noticed the footnote there. If so, you discovered that I based my explanation of Mormon views on the official website of the LDS Church. If I'm going to critique Mormonism, I want to critique what they actually believe, rather than what someone in my tribe says they believe.

Isn't this what I hope Mormon clergy would do for me? Isn't this what we all want from our family, our coworkers, and our church members? How many times have we thrown up our hands in exasperation during an argument, declaring, "But that's not what I'm saying"? We want people to accurately represent us. If they still disagree with us, that's OK, so long as they really understand what we are saying. I work at a seminary, where our students must learn to biblically engage a variety of theological and religious perspectives. To succeed, they will need to describe the "other side" in ways that people on the other side would agree with. This provides persuasion with its greatest opportunity.

In my sermons, I must treat others the way I want to be treated. That involves not just honesty, but humility. Most people are turned off by arrogance. We do not like it at social gatherings, when others turn into what comedian Brian Regan calls the "Me Monster."[11] We do not like it in our date. We do not like it on the job.

Pride is especially repugnant in the pulpit. People expect a preacher to exhibit humility. But it is a fine line we walk. When we preach, we are daring to speak for God. That is an audacious claim, one that should only be made if it is true. Indeed, if our message is biblically faithful and pastorally appropriate, it is

---

[11] Brian Regan, "Me Monster," posted in 2012 by John Doe, 4:16, https://www.youtube.com/watch?v=vymaDgJ7KLg.

true. Preachers are missionaries who speak for God, and we use the Bible to provide a fresh word from the Lord in an ongoing encounter between the gospel and culture.

But in a secular age, many of our listeners on the missional frontier are watching us closely. They want to know if we can preach with authority without being authoritarian. They want to see if the preacher's embodiment of the message compels them to consider its claims.

As those who speak the truth on behalf of God, this is our challenge: to be confident without being cocky, bold without being brash. People do not usually believe the gospel because we have put on a show of force in the pulpit. They are drawn by the mysterious power of the Spirit of God, who uses his Word and our witness. And our witness is most effective when we are most like Jesus.

To preach on the missional frontier, we will need to recover the Beatitudes and the fruit of the Spirit. Preachers will need to exude a different spirit in the pulpit, one that sounds less like talk radio and more like the Suffering Servant.

The Golden Rule of Preaching also requires the most foundational trait of all: love. As my friend Manuel Sosa said, "If I preach on the missional frontier, but do not have love, I am a noisy gong or a clanging cymbal" (see 1 Cor 13:1). Love is essential, because when I preach on the missional frontier, I'm preaching to those who are not yet persuaded.

They may represent all the things that I think are wrong with society.

They may be people you and I would not seek out as friends.

I'll never forget the time a Brooklyn man confessed his crimes during a Bible study in my living room, surrounded by members of our church plant. He was a two-time convicted murderer, he said. I remember my internal reaction, my instinct to reach out and protect my family. But this man lived on the missional frontier, and I had the privilege of preaching to him every Sunday. Only love could compel me to keep preaching to him.

Those who hear our sermons on the missional frontier might struggle with sins that are foreign to us. They may be same-sex attracted, or they may have no regret about their past abortions. They may not value the same things we do. They may struggle with substance abuse, or perhaps they are not sinful but they are homeless. They may not embrace your preferred politicians. The question is, Can you love them, preacher? Can you love them enough to preach the truth in such a way that it connects with them on the frontier of unbelief?

Of course, loving the people who listen to our sermons does not mean we become a pushover in the pulpit. Sometimes, faithfulness to a particular preaching text will demand a firm rebuke, one that some listeners might interpret as harsh or insensitive. There is a time for confrontation. Old Testament prophets knew how to speak truth powerfully. So did Jesus. He was scathing in his denunciation of the Pharisees (Matthew 23). But the same Rabbi who could rebuke the religious leaders of Israel could speak tenderly to a woman in pain (Mark 5:25–34). Threading the needle is important. As America changes around us, we will need to watch our tone and stand unflinchingly for truth.

For most of the last decade, I've been engaged in the richly rewarding, but incredibly challenging work of missional preaching. Some of what I am sharing in this chapter I've learned the hard way. I remember launching a new sermon series centered on the idea of a royal priesthood (1 Pet 2:9). In the introductory sermon, I explained that we were using the concept of priesthood differently than other religious groups. I specifically explained how this was different than the priesthood in the Catholic Church. I don't recall exactly what I said, but I do remember how a single woman in our church was troubled by my statement. She had brought her Catholic boyfriend to church that day, and he protested. He said that what I said didn't accurately represent his experience.

Now, I believe that my theology of the priesthood of every believer was sound (I am happily Protestant). But apparently I stumbled in my explanation. I failed to consider that there could be listeners who would disagree. I did not need to change my theology. But I could have done a better job winsomely and accurately explaining the nuances of doctrine.

By God's grace, sometimes I am able to get it right. Amid a series on sex, I preached a sermon entitled "LGBT: What Would Jesus Do?" I knew a member of our congregation who came every Sunday was struggling with lesbian desires. She was trying to decide whether to embrace life within the LGBT community. I preached what the Bible says about sexuality: It is a beautiful gift that has been created by God to be enjoyed exclusively within the lifelong covenant of marriage between a man and a woman.

I did not water down the message. To do so would have been a betrayal of my sacred duty as a preacher. But in the message, I also spoke with compassion, using a tender tone toward those who might not agree. After the sermon, she came up to me and thanked me. You see, it is possible to marry grace and truth (John 1:14, 17). And when that happens, opportunities for gospel witness abound on the missional frontier. It can start when we learn to watch our tone.

2

Acknowledge the Elephant in the Room

I knew it was going to be a challenging sermon. At our Brooklyn church plant, we were finishing our series through Nehemiah. This small Old Testament book contains a great deal of inspirational material. Texts contain insights about prayer, leadership, confession, and justice. And then there is the ending. The last chapter of Nehemiah tells the story of Nehemiah's reforms. The governor of Jerusalem notes, "In those days I also saw Jews who had married women from Ashdod, Amnon, and Moab. Half of their children spoke the language of Ashdod or the language of one of the other peoples but could not speak Hebrew. I rebuked them, cursed them, beat some of their men, and pulled out their hair" (13:23–25).

This text would challenge our congregation in two ways. First, people would think it odd that Nehemiah assaulted people, and even odder that he pulled out their hair. On the surface, it seems like a bizarre incident of religious hazing. *How weird is that?* Second, the attendees at our church would be unsettled by Nehemiah's motivation. The governor was upset because Jewish men had married non-Jewish women. As a result, their kids didn't all speak Hebrew.

The church I pastored was a multicultural church in a culturally diverse community. Celebrated for its Jewish and West Indian diasporas, the neighborhood of Crown Heights was known for race. It was there that Jackie Robinson broke the color barrier in Major League Baseball when he played for the Brooklyn Dodgers. It was there that the 1991 race riots pitted Blacks against Jews in a terrible three-day melee.[1]

Our multicultural church was situated right in the middle of this historic neighborhood. And when I looked out at my congregation to preach the last chapter of Nehemiah, I would probably see a variety of biracial couples. Over time, our church had been home to Italian–Thai, Malaysian–White, Jamaican–Haitian, and White–Singaporean couples. I knew that when I preached about Nehemiah's reforms, I would probably be preaching to interracial couples.

Such were the hurdles I had to overcome with the sermon. Not only did Nehemiah's actions seem strange, but his

---

[1] See Henry Goldschmidt, *Race and Religion Among the Chosen Peoples of Crown Heights* (Rutgers, 2006).

motivation would no doubt unnerve many of my listeners. They would wonder, *If Nehemiah was upset about interracial marriage, does that mean God is displeased with my interracial relationship?* How do you preach this curious text to biracial couples? That was my challenge, and it was not an easy one.

The final sermon in our Nehemiah series illustrates the conundrum at the heart of this chapter: How do you preach to people who think the text is downright bizarre? If read through a modern interpretive grid, Nehemiah could be seen as a bigoted, violent, authoritarian leader. And yet, the Scripture portrays him as the agent of God in ancient Jerusalem.

I approached this text the same way I try to approach all texts: identify where my listeners are most likely to disagree. Anticipate their objections. Note where they will probably scratch their heads in disbelief. And then prepare a sermon with those skeptics in mind. This does not change the meaning of the biblical text—that was fixed by God! Instead, I'm seeking to develop a more persuasive sermon that is rooted in the meaning of Scripture and engages the anticipated questions of my listeners.

If memory serves, I began that sermon on Nehemiah 13 by acknowledging the elephant in the room. You know about the elephant in the room: It's that topic that everyone knows is there but dances around, whether at the board meeting, in a city council forum, or in a marriage counseling session. The elephant in the room is unpleasant to talk about, so we just awkwardly pretend he is not there. We try to resolve our issues without mentioning the elephant that is eating peanuts in the corner.

In preaching, there is often an elephant in the room. When a biblical text is read at the beginning of a sermon, it will create an emotional reaction: perhaps wonder, anger, or confusion. When something seems strange in a sermon text (like talking donkeys or fighting angels), it suddenly creates an elephant in the room. People are instantly unsettled by the bizarre nature of a Scripture passage. If left to themselves, they will be haunted by the elephant for the rest of the sermon.

It is difficult to listen to a sermon on Nehemiah 13 when all you can think about is what seems like the bigotry and violence endorsed by the text. Do not wait to talk about what your audience is thinking and feeling. Address it at the beginning of your message.

I think what I said in my sermon that day was something like this: "I know what many of you are thinking right now. Some of you are confused. Why is Nehemiah acting this way? And why is he upset because Jews married non-Jews? What's the matter with an interracial marriage? I want to say that I totally get your concern. And I intend to address more fully what this text is doing later in the message. But for now, I just want to say that the point of this passage is religion, not race. Nehemiah is upset because God's people have married practitioners of false religions. And that is the central issue in this passage."

In beginning this way, I let my listeners know that I understand what they may be thinking and feeling. I express that I care about how a message affects them. And importantly, I ask them to suspend judgment for the time being. Did you notice how I promised to later grapple more fully with the question? It was a promise I intended to keep. The elephant had to be addressed directly. But in that moment, I was content to just acknowledge its presence.

When I approach a difficult text, I immediately acknowledge the apparent strangeness of our beliefs. I nod to the elephant in the corner, and then ask people to suspend judgment, just for now. I promise to grapple with the question at the top of their mind before the sermon's end. But I also ask my listeners to embark on a journey with me, to discover whether this text—strange as it is—might really be what they need after all.

In this chapter, we will explore this second strategy for missional preaching. First, we'll see how a biblical hero acknowledged the elephant in the room, then we will explore how one figure from church history did the same. Then, we will end with some practical strategies that answer the following question: How do we preach well when sharing the room with a larger-than-life elephant?

Noah

Noah might seem like a strange candidate for a missional preacher. He was the architect and builder of a massive boat and a rescuer of animals. He was both the keeper of a maritime zoo and a family man who preserved humanity through his children. But a preacher? Noah? Are we talking about the same guy?

Yes, Noah was a preacher. The apostle Peter described the shipbuilder as a "preacher of righteousness" (2 Pet 2:5). Peter applied the same word to Noah that Paul used to describe himself when he declared that he was a herald of the gospel (1 Tim 2:7; 2 Tim 1:11). But what does it mean to be a herald of the gospel?

In the Roman Empire, a herald was an important official who announced royal news. It could be news about the birth of a member of the imperial dynasty or a military victory. It could be the stern warnings that usually preceded war. Julius Kim underscored the importance of the herald when he said that "the herald became the voice of the king."[2] This is the same term that the New Testament applies to those who speak for God. Paul was a herald of the gospel message. He announced the good news of the King. Likewise, Noah was a herald of righteousness.

The Bible doesn't provide the details, but it does give us some context for Noah's "preaching." He lived in an ungodly world (2 Pet 2:5) that was characterized by blissful ignorance. Pre-flood humans lived their lives without thinking about God. He just didn't matter, didn't merit a second thought. Noah's contemporaries ate, drank, and married. They didn't know when God's judgment was coming "until the flood came and swept them all away" (Matt 24:39). Sounds a lot like the modern era!

Noah lived in the ancient world of vice and violence (Gen 6:1–6). The entire planet had become the missional frontier. Amid the chaos and depravity, Noah found favor with the Lord. God extended his unmerited grace to the patriarch and told him to construct a giant rescue vehicle. The ark was designed to house Noah's family and representatives of all the land animals.

---

[2] Julius Kim, *Preaching the Whole Counsel of God: Design and Deliver Gospel-Centered Sermons* (Zondervan, 2015), 19.

But the ark was *huge*. It could have housed more than eight people. Perhaps this gives us a clue to Noah's mysterious preaching. It is feasible that Noah attempted to persuade his neighbors to join him on the ark. Of course, we cannot prove this from Scripture.[3] Yet the Bible does give us two important clues. First, as we have noted, Peter calls Noah a "preacher." That word usually conveys the idea of verbal proclamation. Second, the writer of Hebrews tells us that, by faith, Noah "condemned the world" (Heb 11:7).

Roman heralds often brought a word of judgment on behalf of the emperor. This appears to be what Noah did. He condemned the world by faith. And he had plenty of time for this rhetorical work. Based on the biblical chronology, it appears that it took decades to construct the ark and make it seaworthy. During that time, I imagine, the rumors of the massive boat traveled throughout Mesopotamia. Consequently, he probably fielded many questions. His neighbors were no doubt quizzical. *Noah, why are you devoting your life to this boat?* People throughout the region probably traveled to see the ark with their own eyes. No doubt they asked about its purpose. As one set of writers

---

[3] Although Scripture is largely silent about the nature of Noah's "sermons," a handful of Jewish sources provide some tantalizing possibilities. For instance, the Jewish historian Josephus asserted that, prior to building the ark, Noah attempted to reason with the sinful inhabitants of the earth. If that was true of Noah before he built the ark, it is reasonable to infer that he continued his persuasive efforts while he built it. See Josephus, *The New Complete Works of Josephus*, rev. and expanded ed., trans. William Whiston and commentary by Paul L. Maier (Kregel, 1999), 53.

noted, "The odd structure would undoubtedly have led to questions and answers."[4]

Noah spoke for God at the end of the world (as it was). In the ark, he had an object lesson that provoked wonder, curiosity, and perhaps even ridicule. In fact, it was likely the entire reason that Noah even had an audience for his sermons.

Imagine that people traveled all day from the next village to see Noah's boat with their own eyes. And imagine that Noah, as a preacher of righteousness, began to speak to them on behalf of God. It was a compelling, convicting, and confusing spectacle.

I believe that Noah's sermons must have included warnings of the coming judgment, an explanation for the ark, and an invitation to find refuge. I cannot prove all of that, but I think it is a reasonable attempt to take seriously Peter's description of Noah: preacher of righteousness.

If this is the case, Noah is the classic example of a preacher who had to grapple with his audience's skepticism. It was not a friendly crowd. Noah was not preaching to the choir. And when they saw his grand boat, many of his listeners probably could not keep from laughing. Certainly, many doubted. No one joined Noah on board.

His challenge was to point to the ark and acknowledge how very strange it was. It didn't make sense . . . unless God really had revealed himself to Noah. A boat of this magnitude was strange . . . unless God was about to break into history to do something

---

[4] Dick Lucas and Christopher Green, *The Message of 2 Peter and Jude* (IVP, 1995), 97.

cataclysmic. Devoting your life to an eccentric building project was weird . . . unless a flood was coming.

Preaching at the end of the world, Noah had to speak for God while also acknowledging how strange it all seemed. Perhaps it was that quality of strangeness that prevented any of Noah's neighbors from joining him on the ark. Perhaps they could not overcome their doubt.

For those of us who preach on the missional frontier, that is a lesson all its own. We do not evaluate the success of our sermons based on the response. By that criterion, Noah would have been a failure. If he did give an invitation, nobody came forward. But God numbered him among the faithful (Hebrews 11).

Another lesson comes from Noah's preaching for those of us who dare to speak for God on the frontier of unbelief. As a preacher of righteousness, Noah embodied the message with his life, and he proclaimed it with his lips. An indivisible link connects our witness in the pulpit to our way of life.

Much of life—even our private life—is lived publicly. If I yell at my dog in my backyard, my neighbors hear me. They know when I am rattled; they know when I am angry. All of life is lived before the watching eyes of the world. That is why Jesus called us to be a city on a hill (Matt 5:14–16). If my Sunday sermon is not backed up by Monday morals, then my credibility crumbles, and the sermon loses its power.

Conversely, when our witness outside the pulpit corresponds to our witness in the pulpit, our sermons will radiate moral authority. We will speak as those who have something worthwhile to say. And our listeners—even if they do not believe—will take note.

Noah's listeners certainly took note. They could not help but notice the mammoth vessel that was under construction. I imagine they watched as Noah supervised work teams, putting in long hours for decades. I imagine their curiosity was piqued when a horde of animals passed them en route to the ark. How would you react if you were suddenly surrounded by gazelles, herons, and lions, all of which ignored you because they were migrating to the ark, drawn to it by some mysterious homing beacon?

I imagine Noah's peers watched with rising skepticism as nothing happened for a week. Noah's family and the animals sheltered on board the ark. And the skies were silent. No ominous clouds. No heavy drops of rain. Nothing. Noah's neighbors probably enjoyed a good laugh that week. *Poor old Noah. He is a good man, but he has gone a little crazy in his old age. Poor guy.*

Noah's gossip-producing spectacle sat squarely amid a pile of Mesopotamian soil, collecting dust and derision. Noah's beliefs never seemed stranger . . . until the flood came.

For those of us who live in the progressive city of Portland, it seems like we are preaching at the end of the world. Local leaders promote an agenda that radically rethinks what it means to be human. Education is floundering while violent crime and homelessness have surged in our once-pristine city. On two occasions, our family has even been put on hold when we dialed 911! When Christians preach in Portland, it can feel like we are preaching at the end of the world.

But Noah really was. His message was strange. His methods were even stranger. And I believe that Noah engaged his neighbors with the news he had been given by God. To do so, he would have had to acknowledge the strangeness of his beliefs. Noah must have pointed to the ark, rising above his village, and offered a word of warning. As a preacher of righteousness, this was his vocation: to speak for God at the end of the world.

C. S. Lewis

I recently heard a seven-year-old boy's response to Isaiah's vision of the Lord in his temple (Isaiah 6). "That's strange," he said. The boy was reacting to the fact that, in the vision, the angel put a glowing coal upon Isaiah's lips. I hadn't thought about Isaiah's vision in a while, and as I thought about it, I realized it was a bit strange. That strangeness, this otherworldly character of our faith, is at the heart of our approach to missional preaching. And an ability to acknowledge and then address the bizarre dimensions of our faith (what I'm calling the elephant in the room) is essential for those who preach on the missional frontier. As we struggle with this crucial task, we can turn to an Irish novelist turned British intellectual for inspiration.

C. S. Lewis was an expert in medieval literature who became famous for his fiction and for his works of Christian apologetics. Lewis also delivered around ten sermons during his lifetime.[5] Lewis preached one of those sermons at St. Jude on the Hill Church in London. Delivered during World War II, only weeks

[5] "Lewis as Preacher—a 75th Anniversary Reflection," C. S. Lewis: The Official Website of C. S. Lewis, accessed August 27, 2024, https://www.cslewis.com/lewis-as-preacher-a-75th-anniversary-reflection/.

before the death of Adolf Hitler, "The Grand Miracle" grappled with objections to the Christian faith.

Lewis began by noting that Christians are often asked for a version of "Christianity with the miraculous elements suppressed."[6] As an apologist, C. S. Lewis knew that he had to begin his sermon on miracles by addressing the elephant in the room. He knew that skeptics mocked and doubted the possibility of miracles. Rather than ignore the skeptics, Lewis looked directly at them. He spotted the elephant in the room, and he acknowledged its presence.

Lewis demonstrated a remarkable awareness of other religions as he explained what removing the supernatural would do for both Buddhism and Islam. For Christianity, he claimed, removing miracles would hollow out the religion. Lewis was clear on the high stakes: "The Christian story is precisely the story of one grand miracle, the Christian assertion being that what is beyond all space and time, what is uncreated, eternal, came into nature, into human nature, descended into His own universe, and rose again, bringing nature up with Him. It is precisely one great miracle. If you take that away there is nothing specifically Christian left."[7]

Lewis knew that many of his contemporaries were suspicious of the miraculous. And he knew that the Gospels are full of such stories. Healing a blind man, turning water into wine, the feeding of

---

[6] C. S. Lewis, *God in the Dock: Essays on Theology and Ethics* (Eerdmans, 1970), 80.

[7] Lewis, 80.

the five thousand, the resurrection of Lazarus, and of course, Jesus's own resurrection. And that is to say nothing of the exorcisms Jesus performed. Stories of these power encounters with supernatural beings would have triggered Lewis's most cynical friends!

In beginning his sermon this way, Lewis refused to dodge the issues that give rise to doubt. He refused to preach a safe sermon aimed squarely at the choir. His sermon was printed in a British newspaper and eventually incorporated into *Miracles*.[8] Yet the words we have come to know from a legendary apologetics volume were first uttered at a church. Behind a pulpit. On a Sunday. The words designed to answer the elephant in the room were originally a sermon.

Lewis's approach is reminiscent of another sermon he delivered a year earlier at the Mansfield College Chapel.[9] The occasion was the Feast of Pentecost, and Lewis seized on the chance to explore how God communicates to humanity. Near the beginning of his sermon (called "Transposition"), he shared a confession about the story of Acts 2. Lewis admitted that the spontaneous speaking in tongues practiced by the church on the Day of Pentecost had "often been a stumbling block to me. It is, to be frank, an embarrassing phenomenon."[10]

Preachers would do well to study this model of vulnerability in the pulpit. Lewis acknowledged the elephant in the room. He knew that his contemporaries (perhaps even some in his audience

---

[8] "Lewis as Preacher," C. S. Lewis website.

[9] C. S. Lewis, *The Weight of Glory* (HarperOne, 1980), 18–19.

[10] Lewis, 91–92.

that day) thought that the miracle at Pentecost was unbelievable. So Lewis admitted that he sometimes felt the same way. He had seen the elephant too, and it haunted him.

And yet the strangeness of the biblical story did not dissuade Lewis. He did not deconstruct. He believed. Lewis courageously asserted, "We cannot as Christians shelve the story of Pentecost."[11] If Lewis was not about to deconstruct his faith, why share his struggles in the pulpit?

Poised on the missional frontier, Lewis crafted a sermon that let doubters know that he empathized with them. He, too, thought the miracle at Pentecost was hard to believe! Lewis had doubted, but he held on to the biblical faith.

This missional approach led to a famous passage from Lewis's *Mere Christianity*. He pointed out that Jesus's claims to deity would have seemed to his Jewish neighbors like "the most shocking thing that has ever been uttered by human lips."[12] What do we make of this bold claim? According to Lewis, Jesus presents us with a trilemma. In response to his words, we either believe he is a lunatic, a liar, or the Lord. Those are the options before humanity.[13]

Like Noah, C. S. Lewis preached at the end of the world—or at least it felt like it during the convulsions of World War II. Amid the tumult of a terrible war and a tragic Holocaust, Lewis acknowledged where his listeners might struggle to accept the

---

[11] Lewis, 92.

[12] C. S. Lewis, *The Complete C. S. Lewis Signature Classics* (HarperOne, 1980), 50.

[13] Lewis, 50–51.

biblical story. For him, this usually centered on the miraculous. He knew that his contemporaries doubted the existence of miracles. They had lived through unspeakable horrors, and there were no miracles in sight. And so, in his sermons, he went there. Lewis didn't pretend the elephant didn't exist. He raised the very issue that, for skeptics, was the death knell of Christianity.

Preaching About Elephants

A strange idea lies at the heart of Christianity. We believe that God became man and allowed himself to be executed as a criminal. From the beginning, this message has tripped people up. That is why Paul declared that preaching Christ crucified was a stumbling block to the Jews and foolishness to the Gentiles (1 Cor 1:18–25). The message of the cross still trips people up. As Michael Bird notes, "For critics of Christianity, whether they are Jewish or Greek, ancient or postmodern, the cross is the epitome of religion gone crazy."[14] It helps us preach to skeptics when we consider just how strange our beliefs are. They are only viable if they are true.

Some might propose that we water down biblical teaching, especially the parts deemed bizarre by our neighbors. However, abandoning or tweaking the message is not an option for faithful Christians. Instead of ignoring the unsettling truths of Scripture, we must figure out how to preach about them to those

---

[14] Michael Bird, *What Christians Ought to Believe* (Zondervan, 2016), 117.

who doubt. We must learn to preach about the elephants in the room. I'm certainly no expert, but here are a few practices that I've learned from a decade of preaching on the missional frontier, first in Brooklyn, and then in Portland.

First, we must model authenticity in the pulpit. That's what C. S. Lewis did when he admitted the miracle of Pentecost was hard for him to believe.[15] Those who are Gen Z would have liked Lewis. Liz Lykins makes this point: "In a spiritual context, Gen Z Christians appreciate hearing pastors offer up their own gaps of understanding with Scripture and discuss times they've struggled with their faith or a certain topic."[16]

The emerging generation is looking for preachers who acknowledge how they struggle with the text. Since we all grapple with the text, this should not be that hard. It is a matter of honesty. Those who speak for God at the end of the world must be transparent about their own failures to believe and obey the biblical text. Obviously, this calls for wisdom and discernment, for it is certainly possible to overshare in the pulpit. But many of us tend to undershare. We present ourselves in the pulpit as those who have our act together. We are the preachers who never doubt, the preachers who always submit to the text. And our unbelieving listeners (especially the teenagers in the church who

---

[15] See C. S. Lewis, "Transposition," in Lewis, *The Weight of Glory and Other Addresses* (MacMillan, 1949), 16–29.

[16] Liz Lykins, "Gen Z Christians Want Leaders to Keep It Real," *Christianity Today*, March 24, 2023, https://www.christianitytoday.com/news/2023/march/gen-z-christian-faith-pastors-church-generation-authentic.html.

have not yet believed in Jesus) can see right through us. They cynically pierce the veil of our hypocrisy and decide to seek out more "authentic" voices, usually on social media. What a tragic missed opportunity!

What would happen if we admitted when we do not know what a text means? What if we acknowledged when a text seems strange? What if we confessed our own struggles to obey the text? This sort of countercultural approach to communication is exactly what our younger listeners are thirsting for. As heralds of the good news, our message is gospel-centered, but so is our method. We preach as those who believe what we say. We preach as if we are finite, flawed people who speak for God at the end of the world. We preach as if we are messengers of grace, not of righteous works. We preach as those who can say, "I do believe; help my unbelief" (Mark 9:24). Preaching in the late-modern age requires authenticity in the pulpit. It is the only way to talk about the elephant in the room.

Second, we must preach with pastoral sensitivity. As a pastor of a suburban Portland church, I just finished preaching a series on the book of Judges. Over the course of the series, we plunged into the darkness of the book of Judges. It's a tragic text, replete with assassination, torture, rape, abuse, vandalism, child sacrifice, prostitution, and war. It's the kind of vice and violence that one would find in an HBO drama. The darkness of the story highlights how God's people had become like the Canaanites. The Israelites embraced the Canaanite gods, with disastrous consequences.

In our series, we focused on the theme of idolatry. We asked, "How have we cherished idols in our lives and in our church?"

It was a fruitful series, one that allowed us all to grow deeper in wisdom and in holiness. But it was not without its pitfalls.

Preaching the book of Judges is like driving on a hazardous road. Sinkholes have been known to open up on a major street near our home. We have learned to drive carefully, watching out for unforeseen dangers. Preaching from Judges likewise requires watching out for trouble along the way.

Modern listeners instinctively recoil from the graphic descriptions of violence contained in Judges. Tragically, many modern listeners will be able to relate to what they hear, since nearly one-third of Americans have experienced some form of sexual violence.[17] That means that when we preach about the sexual violence at the end of Judges, our job is that much harder. We are asking traumatized people to enter the darkness of the text because we believe that hope shines even in the dark.

God's Word is not silent about the hard realities of life. It paints an accurate picture of God's people in this era. They were idolatrous, violent, abusive, dishonest, and immoral. Those who don't believe the Christian message find it incredible that the Bible portrays these ancient Israelites as God's chosen people. Yet God does not offer hope to those who are flawless but to those who are fallen. Is that not what is so amazing about grace?

Preaching these texts, however, forces us to grapple with the most honest, accurate self-assessment possible. And it asks

---

[17] Colin Shultz, "Approximately a Third of Americans Have Been the Victims of Sexual Violence," *Smithsonian Magazine,* September 5, 2014, https://www.smithsonianmag.com/smart-news/approximately-third-americans-have-been-victim-sexual-violence-180952626/.

wounded people to stare evil in the eye. This can only be done with pastoral sensitivity and compassion. In our series through Judges, I learned to be discreet with my language, to be tender with my tone, and to be honest about the horrors of the world that are described in the text. And I learned to relentlessly focus on the hope that only Jesus provides.

Noah and C. S. Lewis preached at the end of the world, each in his own way. If we are to preach at the end of the world, our context might seem more like Judges than we would like. But that calls for honesty, courage, and compassion in the pulpit. This is how we preach about the elephants in our cities and in our churches.

Third, we must invite skeptics on a journey of discovery. Preachers tend to feel the pressure to share the gospel in every sermon. That is a good impulse. We preach with urgency because eternity is at stake (2 Cor 5:20–6:2). However, I don't believe that I must preach the entire gospel in every sermon. I believe it is all right to hint at elements of the gospel, without fully elaborating in each sermon. If the gospel is proclaimed through song, and especially through the Lord's Table, then it is possible to leave a sermon more open-ended.

Not everyone will agree with me on this point, and I understand why. We preach Christ, and Christ crucified. But we also preach the whole counsel of God (Acts 20:27). Sometimes, preaching the whole counsel of God will take us to texts (especially from the Old Testament) that do not explicitly articulate the gospel. Rather than force a text to say something that it doesn't, I prefer an inductive approach to preaching that allows the message of a biblical book to unspool itself throughout a sermon series.

When I was a church planter in Brooklyn, I preached inductively through books of the Bible. Sometimes that means preaching a sermon from a text that sounds like a song sung in a minor key. There's no celebration, no triumph, no resolution. This was a palpable tension when our team preached through the book of Job. We called our series "Broken."

In the opening sermon of the series (about Job's first two chapters), I recited the nursery rhyme "Humpty Dumpty" and then threw a raw egg on the ground in front of me. With the mess of a shattered egg before me, I explained that many of us feel like Humpty Dumpty. We're so broken that we think that no one, not even all the king's horses and all the king's men, can put us back together again.

Then I invited my listeners on a journey. I told them that we were all broken, and that we were all wondering if it was possible to be made whole again. I acknowledged the challenges of the text: how Job seems to suffer because of a cosmic wager. In that first sermon, I didn't offer many answers. To those who were doubters, to those who did not believe, I merely invited them to return throughout the series. I invited them on a journey of discovery. I invited them to come with us, to discover if it was possible to be made new. To see if, maybe, *someone* can put Humpty Dumpty together again.

When people are grappling with the elephants in the room (like God's apparent deal with the Adversary in Job's opening sequence), it's important not to rush them. We can't force people to believe, but we can invite them to keep coming. We can invite skeptics to join us on a journey, one that they can quit anytime they wish. But we're inviting them to join us because we believe in the power of the gospel. It changes hearts for it is the power of God unto salvation (Rom 1:16–17). Those who preach about elephants can't use a blunt instrument. They must be persuasive, patient communicators who invite their listeners on what might be a very long journey of spiritual discovery, one that we believe will end with Jesus.

I will never forget one elephant that stared me down while I was preaching in Brooklyn. As our preaching team worked through the book of Colossians, we came to a passage that began with the words "Slaves, obey your human masters in everything" (Col 3:22). It was my turn to preach, and so I had the responsibility to expound this text to our listeners, some of whom were mature Christians, some of whom were young in the faith, and some who had not yet declared for Jesus.

Earlier, I described our multicultural church, which existed in a historic Black neighborhood. And here I was, a white pastor, standing up to speak in a multicultural context about what Paul had to say about slavery. I knew people would feel on edge as soon as the text was read. The elephant in the room loomed large. Our setting only heightened the feeling of angst.

Like many church plants, we were using a rented facility for Sunday worship. We were meeting in a historic performing arts theater, called the Black Lady Theatre. It was started in a previous era by a Black entrepreneur who was frustrated because Black artists were not allowed to showcase their talent in white-owned venues. So, this New Yorker bought his own venue to platform the work of Black artists.

Many years later, on a Sunday morning, as a white pastor of a multicultural church in a historic Black neighborhood, I stood in the Black Lady Theatre to talk about what Paul meant when he said slaves should obey their masters.

I don't know if I said everything just right. I do believe I was faithful to the text and to my context. I invoked many of the strategies outlined in this chapter by acknowledging the angst at the outset of the sermon and addressed the emotions of those for whom the text carried an existential weight. I also invited people to suspend judgment and join me on a journey of discovery, one that I hoped would lead to Jesus. Because, as Randy Alcorn says, Jesus is "the only answer bigger than the questions."[18] Even the questions posed by the elephants in the room.

---

[18] Randy Alcorn, *If God Is Good: Faith in the Midst of Suffering and Evil* (Multnomah, 2009), 206.

3

Narrate the True Story of the World

When I was a kid, my parents carefully selected what I was allowed to watch on television: *MacGyver*, *Jeopardy*, *Star Trek*, and college football. Every year, when I visited my grandparents in Alabama, I was excited at the chance to expand my viewing options to include Saturday morning cartoons. Some of those childhood entertainments continue to influence me today. I still enjoy sci-fi and college football and enjoy sharing those experiences with my family.

My childhood fascination with certain shows was a quest for a story. Everyone loves a good story. That is why blockbuster movies still drop every summer. Streaming services have taken storytelling in new, niche directions. Whether you like romantic comedies or thrillers, open your streaming app and you will find curated lists of movies waiting to be discovered. If you are a sports enthusiast, you can bundle channels that will tell you all the best stories in the world of sports.

People are hardwired to hunger and thirst for good stories. Deep within us, we crave a satisfying story, because we are living out *the* story. Echoes of Eden permeate our lives, resulting in a story-saturated culture. These narratives are experienced collectively, as we connect with others who share our taste in stories. Brett McCracken notes, "Part of why we hunger for the latest Disney princess reboot, the latest Marvel or DC entry, or further movies about the treasured toys of our childhoods is that they invite us into existing traditions and established communities, in ways that make us feel less lonely."[1]

But it is not just content curated by Hollywood. In the era of social media, everyone has a story that can be distributed globally through our favorite apps. Instagram users update their "stories." On TikTok, influencers share brief stories, accumulate millions of followers, and generate reliable streams of income through strategic product placement. Ironically, in our connected, digital, social media–addicted world, people are lonelier than ever. They long to be known, so they go online and share their stories with the world. They don't just want to hear a story; they want to be a part of one.

---

[1] Brett McCracken, "The Longings Behind Pop Culture's Nostalgia Obsession," TGC: The Gospel Coalition, https://www.thegospelcoalition.org/article/longings-pop-culture-nostalgia/.

Followers of Jesus have an answer to both the longing to hear a story and the desire to participate in a story. That answer is the Bible, what two writers have called "the true story of the world."[2] It is nothing less than the unfolding story of God and his action in the world (first to create it, and then to redeem it). This is a grand narrative, the grandest of all. It is cosmic in scope because it begins with creation and ends with new creation. It is a story with explanatory power, one that helps us make sense of our fractured and confusing lives. But many people view this narrative with a large dose of cynicism.

In the twenty-first century, people can either demand a narrative or remain suspicious of stories. On the one hand, some believe in overarching narratives that explain everything. Complicated facets of American society get boiled down to a simple narrative. Politics, race, religion, sports, and entertainment are all assigned roles as "characters" in the grand narratives that we tell. Others are more skeptical about the power of these metanarratives. They worry that we are oversimplifying things, or that we are just telling stories that will prop up those in power.

Regrettably, Christians haven't always done a good job explaining the Bible as the true story of the world. We have analyzed its various parts, slicing and dicing until it has become a collection of disjointed fragments. But what if the Bible is more than the sum of its parts? What if it tells the true story of the

---

[2] Michael Goheen and Craig Bartholomew, *The True Story of the World: Finding Your Place in the Biblical Drama* (Brazos, 2020), 1–6.

world, and what if that is the story that our society has been looking for all along?

Lesslie Newbigin was a British missionary to India who said, "Most of us treat the Bible as an anthology of helpful thoughts to which we may occasionally turn, and from which we can obtain comfort, guidance, direction."[3] He is right about how we approach the Bible. Yet the Bible refuses to be domesticated. It is not something to be caged and let out occasionally when we feel the need for a few spiritual insights. Newbigin said, "It is rather an interpretation of the whole of history from the creation to its end, and of the human story within that creation."[4]

I have the privilege of teaching at a seminary that emphasizes biblical theology. As my colleague Richard Blaylock says, this is "the disciplined pursuit of the meaning of the Bible, both in terms of the meaning of the Bible as a whole and in terms of the meaning of its various parts in relation to the whole."[5] Beginning in Genesis and continuing to Revelation, God reveals himself to humanity through his gracious self-disclosure. He did not have to tell us about himself, but he did, and we are better for it because without it we are lost forever.

The Bible, then, is primarily the story of God, and of his love for the people and the place he created. It contains many diverse stories about angels, animals, and armies. It describes ancient Israel and the early church. It covers both the origin and future

---

[3] Lesslie Newbigin, *A Walk Through the Bible* (Regent, 1999), 3.

[4] Newbigin, 5.

[5] Personal correspondence, February 6, 2024.

of the planet. It is an all-encompassing narrative, "the true story of the world." As Christopher Wright declares, "Through all this variety, locality, particularity and diversity, the Bible is nevertheless actually the story. This is the way it is. This is the grand narrative that constitutes truth for all. . . . This is the universal story that gives a place in the sun to all the little stories."[6]

At the center of this story is a Jewish craftsman named Jesus. He spoke with a Galilean accent and claimed to be the Son of God. Indeed, history demonstrated that he is the climactic message from God to the world in these last days (Heb 1:2). Jesus is the Hero of the Bible's story. He is the hinge around which the narrative turns and the glue that holds all its diverse stories together. Reading the Bible as a narrative means understanding that it is a story centered on Jesus, and we are called to preach that story effectively.

Indeed, we do not have to go far to see that he is the central character of the story. Our word for *gospel* is translated from a Greek word that means "good news." Originally, the word was used to describe the announcement of royal news like the birth of a king, his ascension to the throne, or his victory over rival kingdoms.[7] First-century Christians adopted this word to describe what they proclaimed. They bore witness to the gospel, the good news that the King had been born, had won a great victory over

---

[6] Christopher J. H. Wright, *The Mission of God: Unlocking the Bible's Grand Narrative* (IVP, 2006), 47.

[7] N. T. Wright and Michael F. Bird, *The New Testament in Its World: An Introduction to the History, Literature, and Theology of the First Christians* (Zondervan, 2019), 562–63.

evil (through his death and resurrection), and ascended victoriously to the throne. For the people of God, this was good news.

The announcement of this good news only makes sense in the framework of a story. Indeed, that is exactly what the gospel is. It is the story of how God has acted decisively in history, through Christ, to rescue us from the present evil age (Gal 1:4). Preachers are, above all else, storytellers. We proclaim the gospel by rehearsing the story of Jesus.

You might be concerned by the word *story*. For some, a story is akin to a fable; it is simply not true. In this understanding, a story is distinct from history. I want to be crystal clear: when I refer to the Bible as a story, I understand it as "the true story of the world." Every word of Scripture is true (theologians refer to this concept as inerrancy). The story of Scripture is the faithfully narrated unfolding of God's mission.

Preachers in our post-Christian society would be wise to lean in to the storied nature of our faith. In a society that craves and generates narrative, preachers have an opportunity to preach sermons that are shaped by the unfolding story of Scripture. At the heart of this narrative is One who beckons us to the cross, One who offers hope in a grim world, and One who invites readers to participate in his ongoing story.

Before we explore practical tips for preaching the story, however, we should step back and learn from those who have gone before us. When we do, we will discover that some of the most influential preachers in history have been storytellers, and they proclaimed the true story of the world.

The Apostle Paul

It's tempting to pick Paul as *the* example of everything. He is such a classic figure in the New Testament, and an example of a creative missionary, a stellar theologian, and a gifted writer. When looking for biblical examples of those who preached the story of Scripture, Paul is an obvious choice. Maybe too obvious. In this case, however, he is the right man for the job. Out of all of Paul's sermons, I want to zero in on one of his most memorable: his sermon in Athens delivered on Mars Hill.

Before we talk about how Paul preached the story of Scripture, it is worth exploring the background of this narrative. The apostle Paul never planned to preach a legendary sermon in Athens. He was just waiting for Silas and Timothy. But while he was waiting, he looked around. What he saw got under his skin. Paul observed "that the city was full of idols" (Acts 17:16). He likely saw temples, statues, graves, and sanctuaries. No doubt, he discovered artifacts of the worship of Zeus, Apollo, Athena, Serapis, and Poseidon (to name only a few). Perhaps he stumbled on one of the thirteen altars built in honor of Caesar. Tourists traveled to Athens to appreciate its religious splendor. But Paul was not impressed.

Paul was deeply disturbed by the idolatry that met his eyes. Perhaps it reminded him of how his ancestors had aligned themselves with "lifeless gods," and thereby provoked the Lord to anger (Ps 106:28–29). Now, as he waited among idols, he knew that he must speak up for God.

In contemporary culture, we are overrun with idols. Some of them are obvious. You can drive around your city and note the temples, the mosques, and the shrines of false gods. Other idols are seemingly less religious. Here in Portland, strip clubs and cannabis dispensaries would have provoked Paul's anger. He would have looked at our city and known instinctively what we worship. Other idols of American culture include money, food, identity, power, culture, and government. Those who follow in Paul's footsteps and speak up for God will have to confront the reigning idols of our day. Paul would tell us that it is not easy, but it is the only path for faithful preachers of the gospel.

Paul decided to confront idolatry by telling a better story: the true story of the world (more about that in a moment). After debating with philosophers in the marketplace, he was brought before the Areopagus council, and given a chance to speak on behalf of Jesus. Four hundred fifty years earlier, Socrates had been executed by this same council because of his dangerous ideas. Although Paul was not facing that fate—not yet, at least—the mystique of the place surely loomed large.

Paul's invitation to speak for God in a pluralistic setting reminds me of a unique open mic event I participated in at a park in Brooklyn. In the aftermath of the 2016 presidential election, our majority-minority, deep-blue neighborhood was shocked and angry. The election did not go the way that many of our neighbors had hoped. One of our neighbors was a secular Jewish woman. She was a friend of our family and a key community partner for our church. She asked if I would help organize an open mic event in the nearby park. This was the park our children played in and where our church held summer evangelistic worship services.

I agreed to help, hoping that I could, somehow, make a difference. I was uneasy at the first planning meeting when I realized that I was the only outspoken Christian on the planning team. However, I decided to remain engaged, praying for an opportunity to speak up for God. That came when my Jewish friend asked me if I would deliver prepared remarks at the event. Like Paul, I said yes.

It was a memorable day in Brower Park, as our neighbors gathered to voice their opinions. It was clear that people appreciated the chance to speak up. The setting was pluralistic. My speech was sandwiched between talks delivered by a Muslim and a Buddhist. In some ways, it felt like an odd place to be. After all, as a Christian, I believe there is only one way to heaven, and his name is Jesus. On the other hand, as a missionary/church planter, it seemed like the perfect place to be. I was handed the mic before a crowd of unbelievers and invited to speak for God on the missional frontier. That is what Paul lived for.

I relished the opportunity to speak up for Jesus at the intersection between the gospel and culture. And when I spoke up for Jesus in this angry, pluralistic context, I told stories: the stories of Roger Williams, Martin Luther King Jr., and, of course, Jesus. In the introduction to this book, I said that missional preaching engages people at the frontier of unbelief and invites them to take a journey toward Jesus. Like Paul at Athens, I got the chance to stand on the missional frontier for a few moments and point people toward the Son of God. No miracles of new birth occurred that day, at least not that I know of. But it did give me further chances to engage my neighbors in spiritual dialogue. And I would do that again in a heartbeat. I'm convinced if Paul had the chance to retrace his steps to Athens, he would do the same.

So far, we have explored Paul's pluralistic context, but what about his content? How did he share the story of God before the Areopagus council? Is there anything we can learn about preaching on the missional frontier?

Paul began his sermon by launching into a story, but not the story you would expect. It was not the story of the cross, or the miracles of Jesus, or even the story of Israel in the Old Testament. Paul started his sermon with the story of Athens. One of my church-planting mentors taught me to learn to weave together the story of my city with the story of God.[8] That is what Paul set out to accomplish on Mars Hill. He began by describing what he observed in the city of Athens.

"People of Athens," Paul said, "I see that you are extremely religious in every respect. For as I was passing through and observing the objects of your worship, I even found an altar on which was inscribed, 'To an Unknown God'" (Acts 17:22–23). The introduction to Paul's sermon was a rehearsal of a story that the Athenians knew well: their own. He pointed out the idols that he had observed throughout the city, including one to an "Unknown God." Like a good missionary, Paul had "mapped"

---

[8] Dhati Lewis, *Among Wolves: Disciple-Making in the City* (B&H, 2017), 14–27.

the idolatry of the city.[9] He studied these cultural artifacts and provided a theologically thick description of them. His analysis is the heart of his famous sermon on the "Unknown God."

My thinking about this first-century evangelistic sermon has been shaped by my father's frequent sermons on this text. Paul's sermon at the Areopagus was a favorite for my dad, and I heard him preach and teach on this text many times.[10] According to my father, Paul described the Unknown God as the Creator, the Redeemer, and the Coming Judge. This framework of creation, redemption, and judgment sounds like the story of Scripture.[11]

When Paul was confronted by the repugnant idolatry of Athens, he responded by linking the Athenian story with the story of God. He began by describing God as the Creator. According to Paul, God does not need shrines made by humans, because he is the originator of all things (Acts 17:24). Paul went back to the beginning, to the origin story of the universe. God made the planet ("the world and everything in it"), its people ("he himself gives everyone life and breath"), and its peoples ("from one man he has made every nationality").

---

[9] Caleb Crider, Larry McCrary, Rodney Calfee, and Wade Stephens, *Tradecraft: For the Church on Mission* (The Upstream Collective, 2017), 50–68.

[10] Before he died, my father even began writing a book entitled *The Unknown God*. In the unfinished manuscript, I can still hear his voice as he narrated how Paul told this grand, cosmic narrative.

[11] Osvaldo Padilla, *The Acts of the Apostles: Interpretation, History and Theology* (IVP, 2016), 182, argues that in this sermon Paul uses "a biblical narrative framework moving from creation to judgment."

For people who were used to crafting their own gods, the message of a supreme God who crafted the cosmos would have been dramatically countercultural. Paul was not afraid to be countercultural. He began at the beginning and narrated the true story of the world. God is the Creator. He has spoken. Everything else is a response.[12]

We know instinctively that narratives do not just have a beginning. There is always more to the story, and so Paul continued his sermon by hinting at the redemption offered by the Unknown God. He acknowledged that idolatry had been all too common throughout human (including Athenian) history. However, now God had commanded everyone "to repent, because he has set a day when he is going to judge the world in righteousness by the man he has appointed. He has provided proof of this to everyone by raising him from the dead" (Acts 17:30–31).

The name of Jesus is not uttered in this sermon (although, since Paul was cut off, and never finished his sermon, it is likely he would have spoken the name of Jesus). However, Jesus is clearly present in the sermon. The apostle referred to the man who had been appointed by God to judge the world. Paul said the proof that this man was the appointed judge is his own resurrection from the dead. Someone who has read even one of the four Gospels will immediately recognize the figure of Jesus. This is his story, and he is its hero.

---

[12] J. H. Bavinck, *The Church Between the Temple and Mosque* (Eerdmans, 1966), 18–19.

God acted in history, through Jesus, to redeem us (Eph 1:7). We were dead in our sins, but Christ redeemed us from the curse of the law by living the perfect life we could not live and dying the death we deserved (Gal 3:13). This is redemption, and we must repent and believe to enter the community of the redeemed.

Jesus calls us to repent (Matt 4:17), and Paul did the same. When he pointed to the miracle of Easter and echoed Christ's call for repentance, Paul was immersing himself in the central movement of the biblical story. It is as if Paul had been able to open a Bible, flip to the Gospels, and point to the narratives of Christ's crucifixion and resurrection. Paul already knew that this was the pivotal part of the story. So he crafted his sermon inductively, telling the true story of the world and building to this moment when he unveiled the risen Lord.

For Paul, the story was not yet finished. Easter was a signpost of what was to come. Paul's Unknown God was not simply the Creator and Redeemer; he was the Coming Judge. This speaks to the end of the story: those parts of the Bible that describe the future kingdom and the new earth. We do not know when history will reach its conclusion, but God "has set a day when he is going to judge the world in righteousness" (Acts 17:31).

The apostle wanted to awaken the members of the Areopagus council, to shock them out of their idolatry by warning them of impending judgment. God has appointed a man, he told them, who will stand in judgment over Athens. This future-oriented aspect of Paul's sermon is crucial. A satisfying ending is essential to any good story. The end of the biblical story (what theologians call eschatology) is equally important. The Bible is not a cliff-hanger. It ends just where it is supposed to, with the renewal of all things (Revelation 21–22).

Paul's sermon to the Areopagus council is steeped in the narrative logic of Scripture. He rehearsed the true story of the world, linked it to a local story, and then pointed to the future resolution of both stories. Poised on the missional frontier, Paul embraced his role as a storyteller. He used the framework of the entire Bible to preach the ultimate story, the one that gives meaning to all other stories and subversively fulfills all our idolatrous hopes.[13]

Chrysostom

John Chrysostom was a legendary fourth-century preacher. He pastored in urban Antioch and later served as bishop in the imperial city of Constantinople. The Greek-speaking preacher was nicknamed "Chrysostom," meaning "Golden Mouth," due to "his dazzling effectiveness as a pulpit orator."[14] Chrysostom's sermonic output was prodigious and, incredibly, hundreds of his sermons have survived to the present day. You can purchase the one-volume collection of his sermons on Acts or the three-volume collection of sermons on Genesis (not to mention sermons on Romans, John, etc.). When you read Chrysostom's sermons (usually called homilies), you are listening in on a pastoral conversation that is more than 1,600 years old.

---

[13] Daniel Strange, *Their Rock Is Not Like Our Rock: A Theology of Religions* (Zondervan, 2014), 268–73.

[14] J. N. D. Kelly, *Golden Mouth: The Story of John Chrysostom—Ascetic, Preacher, Bishop* (Cornell, 1995), 4.

Chrysostom preached in settings that sound familiar to the modern ear. He preached amid urban unrest, famine, political conspiracies, natural disasters, and violence. He once preached to a packed congregation while a political asylum seeker hid under the communion table and peeked out at the crowd! He also attracted "educated pagans," making his homilies an early illustration of missional preaching. Contemporary preachers would be wise to learn from the best of Chrysostom.[15]

In his homily on Paul's missional sermon to the Areopagus council, Chrysostom looked to the past and then to the future. In some ways, his sermon mirrored Paul's original message. Chrysostom looked to the beginning of the story, declaring that "to create is God's prerogative."[16] He looked to the end of the narrative with a focus on repentance and judgment. He brought his listeners into the story by noting that Paul's words could have been "to us also."[17] Chrysostom usually preached in a sweeping narrative style that enveloped his congregants in the story of Scripture.

This approach to telling the true story of the world can be seen in Chrysostom's approach to the book of Genesis. In AD 389 he modeled an ancient form of expository preaching as he devoted sixty-seven sermons to the first book of the Bible. Genesis launches the grand narrative of Scripture. Without it,

---

[15] We can also learn from the Preacher's notable failures, like his sinful anti-Semitic rhetoric.

[16] St. John Chrysostom, *The Homilies on the Acts of the Apostles* (Veritas Splendor, 2012), 529.

[17] Chrysostom, 532.

the story is stale and incoherent. Chrysostom understood its importance and preached it as if it were the launch pad for the true story of the world.

Because Chrysostom believed that the Bible was God-breathed, and because he believed it was true, he preached memorable sermons on creation, the flood, Babel, and Abraham. He preached a daily series of sermons that walked through Genesis, verse by verse.

The ancient prince of preachers focused on the details of the text and tried to put his listeners in the sandals of the biblical characters. For example, he noted that Noah was no doubt scorned by his neighbors as he built the ark. They did not have the faith that enabled them to see the salvation that God was offering. Still, Noah persevered. Chrysostom said, "Even though he was not the favorite or darling of any of the human race of the time through his refusal to follow the same route as theirs, nevertheless he found favor in the eyes of the one who haunts the heart."[18]

"Educated pagans" flocked to hear Chrysostom's sermons after a period of civil unrest in Antioch. And although his sermons were aimed primarily at the believers who were listening, Chrysostom engaged unbelievers as well. He anticipated their objections about God's mercy and love as he preached the flood narrative. Chrysostom was committed to faithfully preaching the

---

[18] St. John Chrysostom, ed. Robert C. Hill, *The Fathers of the Church,* vol. 82, *St. John Chrysostom Homilies on Genesis 18–45* (Catholic University of America, 1990), 93.

details of Scripture. He understood intuitively that the narratives of Genesis 1–11 constitute the building blocks of the "true story of the world." And Chrysostom was determined to rehearse that story from the pulpit.

Verse by verse, paragraph by paragraph, episode by episode, Chrysostom preached through most of Genesis. Often he would begin his sermons by reminding his listeners how he had concluded his sermon on the prior day. He would pick up right where he had left off in the biblical text. As he told the foundational narrative of the true story of the world, Chrysostom was committed to maintaining the integrity of the overarching story.

The father of the church never lost sight of the story of Scripture. He knew that the multiple little stories of Genesis were like chapters in a book that ultimately tell one beautiful narrative. The arc of the story, according to Chrysostom, finds its fulfillment in Jesus. He is the point of the story. The pulpiteer made this clear when he discussed the Tree of Knowledge of Good and Evil in Genesis 3. Chrysostom said, "Let us change the topic from the tree to that other one, from this tree to the tree of the cross, and let us see what harm the former caused and what good the latter introduced. . . . The former tree brought death . . . One drove us from paradise, the other led us up to heaven."[19]

Chrysostom's contrast of the two trees reminds me of what one person at our Brooklyn church plant told me. This man had a PhD in English literature. He had taught the book of Genesis

---

[19] Chrysostom, 220–21.

as one of the "great books" of Western civilization, and then he started attending our church in retirement. He was on a spiritual journey and was not shy about disagreeing with my teaching. Since his nonprofit was focused on urban tree care, he commented to me one day that, in his mind, the story of Scripture was centered around trees. The Bible begins with a tree in a garden, ends with a tree in a city, and centers on a tree we call the cross. Chrysostom would have agreed with my friend's framing of the Bible.

For the Greek-speaking preacher, the Bible was true because it was God-breathed. Because it was true, it narrated the only story that really matters. And because it is the only story that ultimately matters, our sermons should be devoted to telling the true story of the world.

The Art of Storytelling

Storytelling is an art. Ask any successful storyteller, from Stephen King to Christopher Nolan. Preachers speak for God in the encounter between the gospel and culture. That means that we tell his story. And if we are going to relate God's story, we should hone our craft.

Sloppy stories are distracting. Have you ever watched the latest installment of your favorite movie franchise only to be disappointed by the poor storytelling? Sometimes new directors try to take the story in fresh directions, only to crash the story on the rocks of the viewer's imagination (*Star Wars*, I'm looking at you).

Preachers proclaim the gospel—an old story of the greatest news. We don't rewrite the story. Instead, we inhabit it and faithfully rehearse it on the missional frontier. As we tell this story, we will discover that the task of storytelling is hard work. That is why preachers must hone the art of storytelling. In the rest of this chapter, we will briefly examine four strategies that could help us to up our storytelling game.

First, we should learn to preach biblical stories as stories. American Christians love the New Testament epistles, or letters. In fact, many American preachers have perfected the science of preaching these books, which are rich in both doctrine and ethics. For the typical American preacher, the epistles are straightforward to communicate. For instance, Paul followed a careful logical progression in the book of Romans, one that can be traced throughout the letter. A careful analysis of Paul's logic will produce a structured outline (usually three points and a poem!) that makes sense to Western churchgoers.

But what about the rest of the Bible? Can we preach the poetry of King David (or of Paul, for that matter) the same way we preach the letters? And what about the stories? Story dominates the Bible because huge swaths of the Scriptures are written in narrative form: Genesis, Exodus, Esther, Joshua, Jonah, the Gospels, and Acts. Not to mention the chronicles of the kings, the judges, and the prophets!

Too often, Western preachers do not know how to communicate biblical narratives. They know how to exegete a text, but they do not know how to tell a story. One of my preaching convictions is that our sermon form should reflect the genre of the text. If we are preaching the Psalms, our sermons should sound poetic, trafficking in metaphor and rich imagery that moves our listeners to sing to God. If we are preaching narrative, our sermons should be crafted to resemble a story.

When we are preaching a biblical story, this should not be hard. We do not need to become running commentaries on the text. We are not commentaries hiding out in the pulpit, but rather we are preachers who speak authoritatively for God. Instead of run-on commentary, preachers who preach biblical narratives should rehearse the story of the text. We should seek to lodge the story within the imaginations of our listeners and then we should bring it to bear upon the contextual challenges that we face (in our church and in our city). That means that a sermon on a biblical narrative should have the feel of a story.

Our listeners on the missional frontier love a good story. Just ask Hollywood, which has mastered the art of storytelling. Fortunately, we are preaching a book that is composed of hundreds of stories. These stories never grow stale, especially when we embrace the shaping power of narrative. When I preached through Galatians recently, I came to a section that could be described as part of Paul's memoirs (Gal 2:1–10). I could break this narrative down into its various parts and create a bullet-point list of truths expressed in this passage. Or I could tell Paul's story. I believe the latter approach is more faithful to the Spirit-inspired form of the text. And so I rehearsed Paul's narrative and then drew implications for how his story ought to shape us. Instead of abstract ideas, preaching biblical stories as stories fosters vivid pictures and concrete realities. It allows us to enter the world of the text.

Second, we should focus on the big story. The Bible is made up of hundreds of stories. But as we noted earlier in this chapter, it tells one overarching story. This is the big story of the Bible: the story of God. As the true story of the world, the Bible relates a cohesive narrative about God's love for the people and place he created.

If we want to connect with skeptical listeners in post-Christian contexts, then we need to learn to tell the big story. We must learn how every sermon text relates to the larger story. Perhaps we are preaching an exilic passage. If so, we must ask ourselves how this text moves the story forward toward Jesus. In preaching this way, preachers must learn to preach about the forest and the trees. They must have a solid grasp of the micro-story (the trees) but also understand its place within the macro-story (the forest).

Our listeners want to know how the stories about Deborah and Rahab, Daniel and Rachel fit within the larger story of Scripture. They wonder too about the non-narrative texts: How do the laws advance the story, and how do poems and prophetic oracles move the plot along? This brings us back, once again, to biblical theology. Preachers must master biblical theology, moving seamlessly between the text and the grand story in which the text is embedded. This is not a call for every preacher to get advanced degrees from seminary (although I do believe seminaries are helpful). It is a call for those of us who are preachers to commit to a lifelong immersion in the storyline of Scripture. We should soak in it until it becomes a part of us.

Balance is crucial. Too much focus on the forest will cause us to miss the beauty of the individual trees. And too much focus on the trees will cause us to miss out on the wonder of the forest. Our non-Christian listeners can tell if we are ignoring the text right in front of us. But they will also insist upon knowing why it all matters. When I preached through the book of Job in Brooklyn, I had to balance the texts before me with the ultimate context of the biblical story. That meant that I often left tensions unresolved, until I arrived at passages like Job 41, where only God can defeat Leviathan. Here, I pointed forward to Jesus, the One who would slay the Dragon. In preaching the story of Job, I must be faithful to preach his story, but I also must situate it within the grander narrative of Scripture, one that centers on Jesus. Ultimately, we are speaking for God on the missional frontier, trying to tell the only story that truly matters.

Third, we should invite our listeners into the story. Earlier in the chapter, I pointed out that, in the digital age, people do not just want to hear a story, they want to be the story. This is why social media is so popular. It gives everyone in the world a platform to tell their own story.

What if the story of God's mission is unfinished? Of course, the inspired record of God's mission is complete. The canon of Scripture is closed, giving us sixty-six inspired books that narrate God's story from Genesis to Revelation. But God is not finished working in the world. He is still active in history through providence, through miracles, and through his church. And he is moving history toward its intended endgame.

In a sense, then, Christians are swept up in this ongoing story of God's rescue mission. We are redeemed and then given a task.

Like Abraham, we are blessed to be a blessing (Gen 12:3). When we communicate the good news on the missional frontier, we are not merely inviting people to intellectually assent to the truthfulness of the story. We are inviting them to place their faith in Christ and to become part of something bigger than themselves.

When we preach on the missional frontier, we get to invite our non-Christian friends to participate in the greatest story the world has ever known. We're not simply offering them an escape to heaven when they die. On behalf of God, we are inviting our listeners to join in what God is doing in the world. Believe it or not, that is compelling to many of our neighbors, who were raised to think of themselves as activists.

The narrative power of Scripture is like drinking hot tea. Tea begins with hot water and some tea leaves, usually in a bag. You steep the tea leaves in the water for about four minutes. Then, when you remove the teabag, you discover that the water has absorbed the color and flavor of the tea leaves. That's how the Bible works. We immerse ourselves in its narrative. We steep in the story of Scripture until our lives absorb the flavor of the Word of God. Then we step into the world as agents of God's mission, people who have inhabited the story and are now playing a role in the ongoing drama of redemption.

Fourth, we should subvert false stories. When we proclaim the true story of the world, we will inevitably undermine the false stories that society likes to tell itself. That is what Paul did in Athens. When he told the true story of the Unknown God, he subverted the false story. He unmasked the idol and exposed it as a lie.

Modern culture tells many stories: stories of autonomy, progress, liberation, and enlightenment (just to name a few). However, the Bible subversively undermines each idolatrous story that we tell.[20] In telling a different story, we will expose the idolatrous narratives of our age. That means unmasking the reigning idols of secular society by humbly and confidently narrating the good news. In Brooklyn, that meant that my sermons unmasked the idolatry of culture and ethnicity. In Portland, that means that my sermons unmask the idols of freedom and pleasure.

Whatever combination of preaching strategies we use, we must focus on telling the true story of the world. It is a story that is true, good, and beautiful, and it's the only story worth telling.

[20] Christopher Watkin, *Biblical Critical Theory: How the Bible's Unfolding Story Makes Sense of Modern Life and Culture* (Zondervan, 2022).

4

Be Ready to Answer

"Christianity is the white man's religion." "The Bible says you can rape your slave." "Paul defends slavery." "Christianity promotes violence." These are some of the many objections I have been given when ministering in places like New York City and Portland, Oregon. I will never forget a sermon I preached from Genesis in Brooklyn. In a series on the life of Abraham, I mentioned that God told Abraham that his descendants would be enslaved in Egypt for 400 years. Immediately after our service concluded, my friend approached me, visibly agitated.

You should know a little about my friend. He was a neighbor of our church, living only a block away. He was a member of the Nation of Islam (though not in good standing). He liked to argue with members of our congregation. He suffered from HIV. And he often came to church slightly intoxicated.

On this occasion, my friend approached me to argue vehemently that the 400 years of slavery were not about the Jewish people in Egypt but about 400 years of slavery in North America. He was reciting a common teaching of the Islamic splinter group known as the Nation of Islam. This Afrocentric sect teaches that Black slavery and oppression in the United States are connected to the story of Abraham.[1]

In response to my sermon, my friend wanted to engage in an extended debate about Genesis, Abraham, slavery, and Islam. At the end of the service, I had to be ready to respond to the arguments of my unbelieving neighbor. While agreeing with him about the horrific, unjust treatment of Africans and African Americans in American history, I had to gently refute his claims about Scripture and about the identity of Abraham's descendants.

This encounter illustrates the crucial link between apologetics, preaching, and the mission of the church. If we preach on the missional frontier, our sermons will inevitably bring questions to the surface for those who listen. Skeptical listeners will wonder about the assertions we make within our sermons. They will fact-check them in real time, using their smartphones, if necessary.

Many people think of apologetics as something that happens on a university campus. For many, it is an esoteric discipline for the elites of society (both inside and outside the church). But as a pastor I do apologetics all the time. It is what I call

---

[1] See Tynnetta Muhammad, "Brief History on Origin of the Nation of Islam," Nation of Islam, March 28, 1996, https://noi.org/noi-history/.

street-level apologetics. The questions I have been pushed to answer come not from the ivory tower, but from the pew. They emerge out of the bodega or the cannabis dispensary. Sometimes the questions are genuine, but sometimes they are just "gotcha" questions. But they always deserve answers.

Members of your church are on the verge of deconstruction. They have heard the counter-stories that undermine Christianity, and they are on the verge of walking away. They have not even told you they are doubting, but they are about to vanish for good. Pastors are called to be good shepherds who care for the doubting and about-to-deconstruct sheep. This means that we must be ready to answer the questions generated by our sermons. But we can do even better than that. By God's grace, we can anticipate many objections and proactively address them in our sermons. We do not have to wait for someone to ask us hard questions. We can embed them within our sermons, demonstrating that Christianity does not shirk the tough issues. In fact, almost all the questions raised by skeptics are already in the Bible.[2]

Writing about the first part of the Bible, Dominick Hernández opines, "Christians are compelled to engage with the text of the Old Testament in a posture that upholds legitimate questions, on the one hand, and prevents unsettled issues from

---

[2] Tim Keller, *Preaching: Communicating Faith in an Age of Skepticism* (Penguin, 2015), 115, asserts, "Your preaching must address the common direct objections to Christianity. Yet even more fundamental than addressing these is to engage with the foundational cultural narratives of your time." This is a profound insight, one that requires careful cultural exegesis.

festering in their hearts like rotten food hidden in the back of a refrigerator, on the other hand."[3] Although he was writing about Old Testament literature, his statement applies more broadly. Our congregants know the challenges that have been leveled against Christianity. If our sermons ignore those critiques, our listeners will think we are out of touch. Worse still, many of them will conclude that the Bible is irrelevant. Their next step will be to walk away from the faith.

For the sake of the sheep, of our secular friends, and of those of different religious backgrounds, we must be ready to answer. Sometimes they will be disheveled and drunk, like my friend in Brooklyn. Other times they will be prestigious scientists, like members of the church I currently serve in Portland. Sometimes they will be the homeless people that I occasionally interact with as I ride the bus to work each day. Whether they are rich or poor, powerful or weak, housed or unhoused, educated or illiterate, they deserve our best gospel answer. Preacher, are you ready to answer?

Peter

On a Thursday night in Jerusalem, a fisherman stood warming himself at a fire. His friend, Jesus of Nazareth, was inside the building undergoing a show trial. Peter was left in the courtyard of the high priest, perhaps attempting to gather details about

[3] Dominick S. Hernández, *Engaging the Old Testament: How to Read Biblical Narrative, Poetry, and Prophecy Well* (Baker, 2023), 9.

what was happening inside. A maid saw Peter and said, "You also were with Jesus, the man from Nazareth" (Mark 14:67). Peter denied his friend for the first time. No doubt he panicked in the moment, and deflected, saying, "I don't know or understand what you're talking about" (v. 68).

Then the maid began to spread the word: An associate of the accused was in the forecourt! Once again, Peter refused to speak up for Jesus. He denied his relationship with the miracle worker. Finally, others in the crowd caught on to his act: "You certainly are one of them, since you're also a Galilean" (Mark 14:70). The impetuous disciple cursed and declared emphatically, "I don't know this man you're talking about!" (v. 71).

The rooster crowed (for the second time) and Jesus looked at Peter. The shame of his betrayal overwhelmed Peter and he broke down in tears. When push came to shove, Peter was not ready to answer.

If Peter's story ended here, it would be a tragic tale with a bitter ending. Thankfully, there is more to the story. Peter's story bears the shape of a beautiful, redemptive arc. On Easter morning, Jesus told the women who first saw him to tell Peter to meet him in Galilee. That meeting occurred on a beach by the Sea of Galilee. Jesus restored Peter and poignantly asked him, "Simon, do you love me?" (John 21:15–19).

Peter answered Jesus, and then he was able to answer the watching world. Years later, when he wrote his first letter to the elect exiles, he urged his recipients to be ready to give an answer. The Christians he was writing to were experiencing some level of social shunning because they were believers. Much like Peter in that chilly Jerusalem courtyard, they had a choice: deny Jesus or speak up for him.

In a now-famous passage, Peter urged his recipients not to be afraid, but to instead be "ready at any time to give a defense to anyone who asks you for a reason for the hope that is in you" (1 Pet 3:15). Perhaps remembering his own shameful moment, Peter urged the elect exiles not to be afraid of those outside of the faith. Rather, they should be prepared to answer the questions that unbelievers put to them. "Be ready to answer." These are watchwords, not just for apologists, but for all those who preach on the frontier of unbelief.

It is fair to ask if Peter ever put his own advice into practice. Did he move from a position of doubt and denial to a place of humble confidence that allowed him to bear witness to the risen Lord? Another way of asking this is to consider whether Peter's preaching demonstrates that he learned how to give an answer. I believe he did, and the proof is in the book of Acts.

Peter preached his first sermon on the Day of Pentecost. It was not planned out in advance but a spontaneous sermon prompted by a string of events: violent wind, tongues of fire, and speaking in tongues. When the first Christians were filled by the Spirit, they immediately began to proclaim the gospel. As Newbigin says, "Mission begins with a kind of explosion of joy. The news that the rejected and crucified Jesus is alive is something that cannot possibly be suppressed. It must be told."[4]

---

[4] Lesslie Newbigin, *The Gospel in a Pluralist Society* (Eerdmans, 1989), 116.

The first Christians burst out of the upper room, and the good news immediately spilled into the streets of Jerusalem. Miraculously, pilgrims from distant lands heard the gospel in their own languages. The Holy Spirit enabled the first Christians to speak in different languages so that the good news would travel to the nations on day one. It was astounding to be able to hear this message in one's own language. It must have also been a bit overwhelming.

Simultaneous gospel witness in Arabic, Hebrew, Egyptian, and Greek (to name a few) blended to create a cacophony. Some bystanders heard the message and understood that something unique had transpired. Some asked a legitimate question: "Look, aren't all these who are speaking Galileans? How is it that each of us can hear them in our own native language?" (Acts 2:7–8). Others sneered and expressed an unfair critique: "They're drunk on new wine" (v. 13).

The apostles stepped into the chaos to address the murmuring crowd, and Peter took the lead. His first sermon was not the result of careful study in a church office. Peter's first sermon was an answer to a question and a response to an accusation. By the power of the Spirit, Peter was ready to answer. This is street-level apologetics at its finest.

Peter began by saying, "These people are not drunk, as you suppose, since it's only nine in the morning" (Acts 2:14–15). He then unpacked the ancient prophecy recorded in Joel 2 about the last days. Long ago, Joel had foreseen that the Spirit would empower the people of God so that they could bear witness to the Lord in miraculous ways. Peter explained that Joel's prediction had come true, right before their very eyes.

This was not intoxication. It was a miracle, one that had been a long time coming. After deftly explaining the significance of the day's events, Peter pointed his listeners back to Jesus. He explained that Jesus had been the point all along. Peter swiftly narrated the story of Jesus: his life, death, and resurrection. He then announced, "Therefore let all the house of Israel know with certainty that God has made this Jesus, whom you crucified, both Lord and Messiah" (Acts 2:36).

In a fascinating twist, this sermon was not entirely a monologue. Peter's listeners responded with a question. "When they heard this, they were pierced to the heart and said to Peter and the rest of the apostles: 'Brothers, what should we do?'" (Acts 2:37). Nearly two months earlier, Peter had stumbled badly when a maid asked him a question by a fireside. Now, transformed by the Spirit, he was ready to answer: "Repent and be baptized, each of you" (v. 38).

The missional frontier came to Peter that day, and he stood confidently on that frontier to deliver the gospel that Jesus had entrusted to the apostles. And as we know, 3,000 people embraced Jesus as Lord and Messiah that day. All because Peter was ready to answer.

But this was not a one-off event. Peter was ready to answer again when a miracle occurred on the outskirts of the temple. One afternoon, he and John went to the temple to pray. They encountered a paralyzed man (he had been disabled since birth) who was begging for money. Peter and John answered his question by giving him something better than what he sought. In the name of Jesus, they restored his body, and within moments he was dancing around the temple, giving praise to God (Acts 3:1–10).

Unsurprisingly, this miracle sparked wonder in the surging crowd: "All the people, utterly astonished, ran toward them" and congregated on Solomon's Colonnade (also known as Solomon's Porch), at the edge of the temple (Acts 3:11). If you suddenly heard that miracle workers had healed a man who had suffered for a lifetime, you would probably also run to the scene of the action. With the throbbing crowd before him, Peter stood on Solomon's Colonnade and asked a question of his own: "Fellow Israelites, why are you amazed at this? Why do you stare at us, as though we had made him walk by our own power or godliness?" (Acts 3:12).

Peter had learned that sometimes the best answer to a question is simply asking another question. Once again, he pointed his listeners to the crucified and resurrected Messiah. Peter clarified that it was faith in Jesus that had given the paralyzed man his health, for the first time in his life. He wove in and out of Old Testament exposition while explaining that Jesus was the climax of Jewish history, the One they had gathered at the temple to worship.

The response to Peter's impromptu missional sermon was fierce: "While they were speaking to the people, the priests, the captain of the temple police, and the Sadducees confronted them" (Acts 4:1). Irritated at the apostolic witness to the resurrection, the Jewish religious leaders promptly arrested Peter and John. This is a lesson all its own. Sometimes missional preaching prompts a backlash. Sometimes we will suffer when we speak up for Jesus, but we do it anyway because our God is worth it. Peter was willing to answer because he had met the risen Lord on the shores of the Sea of Galilee. Now he would follow him anywhere, even to prison.

And yet there was another response to Peter's sermon: "Many of those who heard the message believed, and the number of the men came to about five thousand" (Acts 4:4). The church pulsated with new life because of the missional preaching of people like Peter.

Peter had been transformed from a fearful friend to a courageous prophet. Having failed and been restored, he had learned how to be ready to answer the questions that non-Christians put to him. Somewhere on the missional frontier, those who listen to our sermons are wondering whether anyone will answer their questions. Our neighbors have posed the question, and now they are waiting for our answer.

D. T. Niles

In 1871, Henry Ward Beecher delivered a series of lectures at Yale Divinity School, launching the annual Lyman Beecher Lectureship on Preaching.[5] For nearly a hundred years, the lecturers hailed from the Western world. In 1957, Yale finally heard a voice speaking up for God from the other half of the world.

---

[5] See "Lyman Beecher Lectures," Yale University Library: Divinity Library, accessed August 27, 2024, https://web.library.yale.edu/divinity/beecher-lectures.

Daniel Thambyrajah (D. T.) Niles, a Methodist leader, was from Sri Lanka (then called Ceylon).

Niles was a noted Methodist evangelist, pastor, and denominational leader. He wrote books about missions and evangelism, and he delivered three sets of lectures on preaching (in Australia, the United States, and Scotland). In April 1957, Niles delivered an unparalleled series of talks about missional preaching. He spoke eloquently at Yale about "The Preacher's Task and the Stone of Stumbling." These talks have come down to us (with some modest additions) as a book that bears the same name.[6]

Before exploring what Niles had to say, it is important to point out that he was, like every figure (other than Jesus) profiled in this book, a sinful person with imperfect ideas. Not all his beliefs will resonate with evangelicals. As an evangelical myself, I resist his ecumenical impulse and especially his pull toward soteriological inclusivity. Still, Niles had some remarkably biblical insights about preaching, especially when he delivered the Lyman Beecher lectures in 1957. If we submit ourselves to the authority of Scripture and use it as our filter, we can charitably listen to and discerningly appreciate the words of Niles as they echo into the twenty-first century.

D. T. Niles preached on the missional frontier. He ministered in a country in which Christians were a tiny minority, and he refused to merely operate within a holy huddle. As a Christian leader, he was both inward-facing and outward-facing. Internally,

[6] D. T. Niles, *The Preacher's Task and the Stone of Stumbling: Proclaiming the Word of God to a Searching Generation* (Harper, 1958).

he sought to strengthen the church regionally and globally, but he was rooted in his own ministerial context. Externally, he pursued friendships with people of other religious backgrounds.

Niles was a product of the missionary encounter between the gospel and culture (his grandfather was one of the first converts from his people group). He was immersed in the missionary encounter. For Niles, preaching always occurred on the frontier of unbelief. It was this dynamic missionary encounter between the gospel and the religions of Sri Lanka that made his lectures so compelling.

In preparation for his lectures, Niles corresponded with three friends: one Hindu, one Muslim, and one Buddhist. He asked each of them to write him a letter indicating what central idea of Christianity caused them to reject the Christian faith. And when they graciously responded, he then incorporated that feedback into his lectures. In the ivory towers of Yale, the missionary-preacher demonstrated how to preach the incarnate God (to Hindus), the crucified Christ (to Muslims), and the risen Lord (to Buddhists). To use Peter's words, Niles was ready with an answer for his friends.

"God has acted and men must believe," Niles declared. "That is the ground of the preacher's task. But men find in this action of God something they stumble over. That is the heart of the preacher's problem."[7] The missional preacher understood that his Hindu, Muslim, and Buddhist friends were stumbling over the

[7] Niles, 11.

person and work of Jesus. Each of his lectures was a response to the challenge.

To his Hindu friend, Niles responded to critiques about eternal judgment (contrasted to reincarnation) and the unique revelation of God through Jesus. Hindu people readily declare themselves at home with Jesus. Portraits of Jesus can sometimes be found in Hindu temples, because he is viewed there as one of many gods.[8] Yet the Galilean Rabbi refused to be labeled as just "one of the gods." According to Jesus, he was (and is) the I AM (John 8:58).

Niles understood that answering the objections of his Hindu friend required preaching Jesus as the incarnate God. Because Hindus embrace the doctrine of reincarnation, they believe that history is meandering and cyclical. But the incarnation is the Creator's invasion of the cosmos. It is a unique irruption in time. Niles declared, "The Hindu needs no doctrine of redemption within history. The Christian is lost without it. That is why the Christian faith insists that the Incarnation, the Cross, and the Resurrection are not only acts of revelation but also of redemption."[9]

The Sri Lankan evangelist believed that those who preach to Hindus must emphasize the incarnation. Theologically, it is one of the decisive points of the biblical story. Tactically, it is also the key to engaging those who believe they are trapped in a

---

[8] Lesslie Newbigin, *The Gospel in a Pluralist Society* (Eerdmans, 1989), 3.

[9] Niles, *The Preacher's Task and the Stone of Stumbling*, 32.

seemingly endless cycle of reincarnation, in a cosmos they believe is teeming with millions of gods.

If the incarnation must be emphasized when preaching to Hindus, the crucifixion must be emphasized when preaching to Muslims. Niles made this point in response to a letter from his Muslim friend, who declared that he rejected Christianity because he believed that Jesus was not God. Muslims usually have a high regard for Jesus, because they believe he was one of the prophets of God. Like Niles's friend, they do not believe that Jesus was the Son of God (the idea of the Trinity is repulsive to Muslims, who believe that Christians are tri-theists).[10] Muslims also strenuously object to the crucifixion of Jesus. In short, they believe Jesus was not God and that he did not die on a tree.

Niles knew that Islam was fundamentally different from Christianity because it allowed humanity to try to attain some level of righteousness apart from divine intervention. He understood that Islamic thinking depends on following the moral teachings of a long line of prophets (including Jesus and culminating with Muhammad). But Christianity does not teach that we can successfully live up to the moral standards of any prophet, especially Jesus. The Bible uniquely declares that paradise has been lost due to our sin, and only God's entrance into the world, and his death on our behalf, can make us right with God. Niles poignantly declared that, in Jesus, "Paradise had been planted in human history."[11]

---

[10] A. S. Ibrahim, *Reaching Your Muslim Neighbor with the Gospel* (Crossway, 2022), 76–85.

[11] Niles, *The Preacher's Task and the Stone of Stumbling*, 47.

In preaching to those from other faiths, it is tempting to downplay our disagreements. For instance, preachers who engage Muslims might prefer to emphasize how we both think Jesus is a prophet of God. However, Niles cautioned us that we cannot merely present the Jesus who will be received by our listeners; we must present the Jesus of the Bible. It is true that our Muslim listeners stumble over the idea that God had a Son who died on the cross. It is up to us, then, to answer their objections in our preaching.

That means we cannot avoid complex topics like the Trinity. As Niles said, "The indescribable mystery of the Trinity is something we cannot escape, precisely because something has happened to us in Jesus Christ which we cannot deny and which we must make meaningful to others."[12] If our listeners trip over the idea that God is both three and one, then we must take the time in our sermons to carefully explain the Trinity: both what it means and what it does not mean. Ultimately, Niles believed that preaching to Muslims (and to all people, for that matter) means preaching Christ crucified (1 Cor 1:23).

The last letter that Niles incorporated into his Lyman Beecher lectures was from a Buddhist friend. This friend objected to Christianity on multiple grounds. But his most straightforward argument was that Christianity emphasized "foreign intervention," but Buddhists believe in merit-based karma. Without using the word, the Buddhist letter writer showcased the centrality of grace to Christianity.

---

[12] Niles, 57.

Niles responded, "It cost God an incarnation and a crucifixion to be gracious to man. But more than that, it cost a resurrection to remain gracious."[13] If Buddhists doggedly pursue enlightenment and release through the Eightfold Path, then they have little room for grace.[14] Yet grace is at the heart of what it means to live as a follower of Jesus. As Niles asserted, "The good news of grace that the Christian preacher proclaims is the good news that Jesus Christ is risen from the dead."[15]

For those who are struggling to live up to the high ideals of Buddhism (no premarital sex, no alcohol, no rudeness, no lying, etc.), Christianity offers a liberating alternative.[16] The Bible contains the highest moral standards of any world religion. Yet it also tells us that we will fall short of that requirement (Rom 3:23). In fact, that is the entire point of the gospel story. Jesus came to live the perfect life that humans could not live, and to die the death that we deserve (Rom 6:23).

D. T. Niles believed that the resurrection of Christ unleashed an era of grace that changed the world. Jesus is the risen Lord, who offers a word of grace to those who do not deserve it. For Buddhists on the difficult path to enlightenment, this is good news.

---

[13] Niles, 75.

[14] John Dickson, *A Doubter's Guide to World Religions* (Zondervan, 2022), 280–81.

[15] Niles, *The Preacher's Task and the Stone of Stumbling*, 76.

[16] "Episode 73: On Buddhism," with Kanishka Raffel and Sarah Shaw, *Undeceptions* (podcast), https://undeceptions.com/podcast/on-buddhism/.

The lectures that Niles delivered were not faultless. I would certainly take exception to some of his claims. But the central genius of these lectures was Niles's demonstration of how preaching can answer objections from rival religions. Peter would have appreciated how the Sri Lankan preacher humbly but confidently engaged his Hindu, Muslim, and Buddhist friends with the unchanging good news of Jesus. Niles was able to pull it off without sidestepping the hard questions or watering down the message of the cross. He declared, "Christianity needs to learn not only the lesson of neighborliness with respect to other religions, it also needs to learn the lesson of maintaining at the center of its own life that gospel of grace which is the judgment on all religions."[17]

Ready, Set, Go?

All this talk about doing apologetics in our sermons can feel overwhelming, even to the most bookish preacher. So, where do we start? Are there any tips everyday preachers can implement on day one? I believe we can take at least three simple steps that will enable us to be ready to answer. Think of them as a posture, a practice, and a pathway.

First, we must adopt the posture of a perpetual student as we learn to anticipate objections to the Christian faith. This is related to what we discussed in chapter 2. However, in that chapter we talked about internal issues: acknowledging the elephant

---

[17] Niles, *The Preacher's Task and the Stone of Stumbling*, 77.

in the room (where the elephants were metaphors for strange or confusing elements of the biblical text). In this chapter, the focus has been on external issues that will arise, not so much from within the Bible, but from the hearts of our listeners.

Everyone comes to church with a bias. The culture in which we live cultivates us. It curates our loves, fosters our idolatries, and limits our ability to see the truth as it really is.[18] Because of the effects of sin, those who hear our sermons will likely already have a default set of objections to Christianity (even if they are believers, they may struggle with some of these issues). It is almost impossible to live in the United States and not be aware of some of these objections. With the proliferation of voices on the internet, critiques are coming in from all sides.

As missional preachers, we must anticipate those objections through diligent study. We should at least sample the media (magazines, social media feeds, music, and movies are a good place to start) consumed by the people we are trying to reach. We should read and watch material produced by critics of Christianity. You do not have to become an expert on what everyone everywhere thinks about Christianity. But you should know what sorts of arguments the people you preach to are hearing and reading. We need to discipline ourselves for the hard work

---

[18] Of course, there are also many reasons to appreciate culture (starting with the fact that God created culture and told humans to steward it). It is not my intent to foster a combative attitude toward the world outside of the church. The unbelievers around us (including those who hear our sermons) are neighbors to be won, not enemies to be defeated.

of cultural exegesis, which enables us to anticipate the objections that will likely be raised by the people we serve. This requires the posture of a student.

Second, we must adopt the practice of civility. This relates to what we covered in the first chapter about watching our tone. Too many Christians get excited about apologetics because they view it as an opportunity to debate and defeat non-Christians. But Peter pumps the brakes on our desire to "own the other side."

It is true that he calls us to be ready to answer, but he makes it clear how we are to answer: with gentleness (1 Pet 3:16). The Greek word that Peter used can be translated as "gentleness," "humility," "courtesy," "considerateness," or "meekness."[19] Some modern-day Christians are ready to answer . . . with bombast and ridicule. They almost never persuade anyone.

If we are serious about persuading people, then it is time we listened to Peter. We must adopt the practice of civility. The church I serve in suburban Portland recently launched a class called "Confronting Christianity."[20] In our first session, we had a mixed audience: There were mature Christians, young Christians, and non-Christians in the room, so it was important to establish two ground rules.[21] I said that every question was fair game in

---

[19] Walter Bauer, *A Greek-English Lexicon of the New Testament and Other Early Christian Literature*, rev. and ed. Frederick W. Danker, 3rd ed. (University of Chicago Press, 2000), 861.

[20] Based on the excellent book by Rebecca McLaughlin, *Confronting Christianity* (Crossway, 2019).

[21] See Sam Chan and Malcolm Gill, *Topical Preaching in a Complex World* (Zondervan, 2021), 72–77, for excellent suggestions about how to communicate to both believers and unbelievers at the same time.

the class. I encouraged those who were skeptical to bring their doubts to the table, and I promised them that they would not be canceled for airing their views.

Then I said that the Bible would be the final authority for all questions discussed in the class. I tried to position our class as a cadre of pilgrims on an intellectual quest. But our quest was rooted in the church's commitment to the authority of Scripture. Ours was a faith that was seeking understanding (to paraphrase Anselm). If skeptics are truly welcome in our midst, they must be made to feel welcome. That starts when we adopt the practice of civility.

Third, we must walk the pathway of hope. Peter wanted his readers to be ready to give an answer about their hope (1 Pet 3:15). Maybe he floundered by the fireside when confronted by a maid because, on the eve of the crucifixion, he had no hope. But in the aftermath of Easter, hope was a viable alternative.

Missional preachers explore how the gospel serves as a wellspring for hope, one that bubbles up into our lives in even the darkest of times. This is how we are ready to answer. We live lives suffused with hope, and then we connect the dots for our listeners. We explain from the Scriptures that Jesus is the source of our hope. Through his life, death, and resurrection, he has initiated a revolution of hope in a world of despair.

This hopeful way of life does not mean that preachers magically have all the answers. Sometimes being ready to answer means admitting you may not be sure of *how* to answer. Missional preachers must cultivate and radiate hope. We do that by answering as many questions as we can and by pointing to the One who is the ultimate answer. We invite our listeners to join us as we tread the pathway of hope in a weary world.

Peter and D. T. Niles would both want us to provide answers in our sermons—not with bombast and hubris, but with gentle confidence and unshakable hope. That's what happens when a preacher stands on the frontier of unbelief and is ready to answer.

5

Celebrate Truth, Goodness, and Beauty

I did not want to preach on Ecclesiastes, but I was outvoted. At our church plant in Brooklyn, after prayerful consideration, our leadership team decided we were going to preach through Ecclesiastes. I was disappointed. I knew it would be hard, because, well, it is Ecclesiastes. Interpretive and homiletic challenges abound in this ancient book. But our leadership team believed that it was just what we needed. I submitted to the group's decision, even though I disagreed, and it turns out that I was wrong.

I got to work crafting a sermon series called Chasing the Wind because every New Yorker has a hustle. To afford the ridiculously high cost of renting a tiny, cramped apartment, New Yorkers work multiple jobs. They are always running. Sometimes they are chasing their dreams: move to New York City, wait tables, and then become a Broadway star. Sometimes they are international students, pursuing the opportunities of higher education in America. Sometimes they are just everyday people who are working side gigs to pay rent and order takeout every night (a cherished way of life for many New Yorkers). As a result, our neighbors were always hustling. Literally. Head down, speed-walking toward the train station.

In the words of Solomon, we are enmeshed in life under the sun. And the good life always seems just beyond our grasp. But we are so close, we can almost taste it. That is why New Yorkers chase the wind.

At about the same time, a young woman began attending our Sunday gathering. She was a Christian but had experienced a form of deconstruction, and her faith took a hit. Now, years later, she was back at church to reconnect with God and renew her faith. She underwent a remarkable spiritual transformation over the course of a few years as she pivoted her life back to God. Later, she wrote in a neighborhood magazine that our sermon series on Ecclesiastes had been instrumental in helping her rediscover Jesus.

I was floored. Our "Chasing the Wind" series was the toughest sermon series we had ever done. Sometimes I wondered if we were accomplishing anything of eternal value. (Perhaps I had imbibed some of Solomon's skepticism!) But with the perspective that comes from hindsight and first-person testimony, I realized that Ecclesiastes was just what the doctor had ordered.

Solomon's enigmatic book grapples with how to find the good life under the sun. It pings between despair at the futility of life and celebration of beautiful things, like food, drink, and friendship. The entire book is also anchored in truth claims: There is a Creator, and humans were made to fear him and keep his commands.

Our series connected with our neighbors because Ecclesiastes pulls at the trio of threads that are interwoven into our lives: truth, goodness, and beauty. I am convinced that those who preach on the frontier of unbelief need to embrace a style of preaching that celebrates all three.

As evangelical preachers, we take it for granted that the message we preach is true. Some of those who hear our sermons are not so convinced. Still, as we learned in an earlier chapter, we preach "the true story of the world." But it is not only questions of truth that trip up our listeners. In the late-modern age, people frequently object to Christianity on the grounds of goodness and beauty.

On Good Friday in 2022, I had the privilege of preaching at the church plant in Northeast Portland that my family attended. The Russian invasion of Ukraine had launched just under two months prior. Daily, we were treated to horrific stories and pictures of the unjustly attempted conquest. I knew there were unbelievers in attendance that night. I also knew that many of us would be struggling with the goodness of God in the context of war, so I decided to look to the cry of dereliction for hope.

The cry of dereliction is the phrase that theologians use to describe the anguished cry of Jesus from the cross: "My God, my God, why have you abandoned me?" (Mark 15:34). To those who were doubting God's goodness, I shared this anguished cry, and we trembled together on the edge of this mysterious moment. This word from the cross demonstrates that Jesus understands our pain because he became sin for us. This is good news for suffering sinners like us. We can relate to the feeling of loss and the sensation of pain. On Good Friday in 2022, with war raging in Europe, God met the challenge to his goodness and answered with the cross.

Beauty is even harder for many evangelical preachers to grasp. It is not so much that we do not know what is beautiful. Rather, we do not always appreciate it. But our secular neighbors do appreciate beauty, especially in a darkened age characterized by addiction, disease, violence, corruption, and unemployment. My job as a preacher in an age of despair is to narrate a beautiful story about a beautiful God who has acted in history to save us from this darkness.

Speaking on the task of apologetics, Gavin Ortlund declares, "Many modern people are not even *interested* in whether the gospel is true. We have to start further back, helping people understand why the gospel is worth considering in the first place. To this end, the beauty of the gospel is a profoundly useful tool. It can cut through apathy to arrest the attention of our hearers."[1] What is true of apologetics is also true of preaching on the missional frontier. When our listeners are profoundly amazed by the beauty of Jesus, they will often be drawn to the good life he

---

[1] Gavin Ortlund, "Apologetics in an Age of Despair," TGC: U.S. Edition, June 12, 2023, https://www.thegospelcoalition.org/article/apologetics-age-despair/.

offers and submit to the truth that he embodies. Our challenge is to preach in such a way that our non-Christian listeners are dazzled by the person and work of Jesus. For those of us who are trained in a pragmatic way of viewing the world, this requires a course correction.[2]

Paul Gould notes, "Reason guides on the quest for truth. The conscience leads us to goodness. And the imagination transports us toward beauty."[3] Missional preachers must learn how to engage the mind, the conscience, and the imagination of those on the frontier of unbelief. Preaching at its best has always done this. And that should not surprise us. After all, the Bible is the true story of the world. It is the pathway to human flourishing (the good life). And it creates outposts of beauty amid the rubble of our world. Our preaching should embrace the ancient triad of truth, goodness, and beauty, for our God is the embodiment of all three.

Ezra

What is the longest sermon you have ever heard? What is the longest sermon you have ever preached? Chances are, no preaching experience you have ever had compares to Ezra's epic

---

[2] See Stephen Stallard, "The Beautiful Journey: Art and the Mission of God," Center for Faith & Culture, March 22, 2021, https://cfc.sebts.edu/faith-and-culture/beautiful-journey-art-mission-god/.

[3] Paul M. Gould, *Cultural Apologetics: Renewing the Christian Voice, Conscience, and Imagination in a Disenchanted World* (Zondervan, 2019), 29.

sermon in Jerusalem. Nehemiah the governor had just led an emergency program to restore the walls in the face of threats from external enemies. Now, with the walls rebuilt and their enemies safely at bay, God's people gathered to hear from God. Ezra the priest opened the Torah and read it "from daybreak until noon" (Neh 8:3).

A team of preachers worked alongside Ezra during this lengthy worship service. Thirteen Levites "explained the law to the people as they stood in their places. They read out of the book of the law of God, translating and giving the meaning so that the people could understand what was read" (Neh 8:7–8). Reading between the lines, here's what I imagine: Ezra would read a portion of the Torah, and then the Levites—scattered throughout the crowd—would explain that portion of the text to those around them.

Ezra and his team of preachers engaged the minds of the Israelites. They read the law and explained its meaning. The initial goal was comprehension: "so that the people could understand what was read" (Neh 8:8). We have all probably experienced what it is like when we do not understand a biblical text. We feel like the Ethiopian eunuch, who said that he could not understand the Word of God unless someone guided him (Acts 8:30–31).

Ezra and the Levites reintroduced the Torah to God's people at a fresh moment in their history. They had been enslaved and exiled but had now been granted the right of return. They were rebuilding the city, but now they needed to rebuild themselves. This required the Word of the living God. In this vulnerable but exciting moment, the Israelites heard God's voice through the law. But to ensure maximum impact, the group of preachers patiently explained the law . . . all morning.

Most preachers intuitively understand this aspect of the task of preaching. They know that they are called to explain God's Word to God's people. In this way, we carry on in the spirit of Ezra (and of Jesus, who did the same thing in Luke 4). When we preach on the missional frontier, we must engage the minds of our listeners. We must embrace the intellectual dimension of our work as preachers. We study the Bible and explain its meaning to God's people.

But that is not all that Ezra did. He also engaged the conscience of the Israelites. That is evident in their response: They wept as they heard the Word of God (Neh 8:9). God's people recognized that they had not lived up to their vocation as a kingdom of priests that served as a light to the nations (see Exod 19:5–6). Having been exiled by God, they now had a fresh chance to follow him in the land of their ancestors.

When the Israelites held up the Word of God as a mirror, they did not like what they saw. It challenged them and made them uncomfortable. Ezra explained the Torah as the key to flourishing in the Promised Land. If God's people were going to live the good life, they would have to abide by the terms of the covenant. This unsettled God's people. They were haunted by Scripture.

The Bible is not merely a book with words on a page. It does something because it is living and active (Heb 4:12). Good preaching also focuses on *doing* something, not just transmitting information. In the act of preaching, we prick the conscience and engage the moral dimension of our listeners. Using the Scriptures, we point to the pathway for human flourishing. When we aim for the good life (as defined by God), we are entering the arena of goodness.

Ezra was not content with the explanation of God's Word. He was after a moral transformation. Those who preach on the missional frontier must embark upon a quest for gospel-centered transformation. We are aiming, not just for the head, but for the heart and the hands as well. Like Ezra, our hope is that the Holy Spirit will use God's Word, crashing like a wave over our souls, and with it will produce within us authentic goodness.

Finally, amid Jerusalem's urban renewal, Ezra and his team of preachers beckoned toward beauty. This is the final element of the ancient triad: truth, goodness, and beauty. The leaders of Israel instructed God's people: "Go and eat what is rich, drink what is sweet, and send portions to those who have nothing prepared, since today is holy to our Lord. Do not grieve, because the joy of the LORD is your strength" (Neh 8:10).

Ezra saw a recovering city with a rebuilt wall and a repentant congregation with renewed worship. And he preached on joy. As one writer notes, "The order may seem upside down to certain Christians, who are so aware of their unrighteousness that they wallow in their unworthiness."[4] But Ezra understood that God's people, realizing their own inadequacy in the face of the law, were filled with shame. The priest responded by urging people to celebrate God's gifts: rich food and sweet drinks.

---

[4] Dean Ulrich, *Now and Not Yet: Theology and Mission in Ezra-Nehemiah* (IVP, 2021), 131.

Beauty is impossible apart from grace. God gives to us "gratuitously," out of his great love, and the beauty of creation reflects the perfect beauty of the Trinity.[5] The new wall around Jerusalem probably wasn't fancy. But I guarantee you it was a beautiful sight to the embattled refugees of the city. And now, given permission from their leaders, they could taste and see that the Lord was good (Ps 34:8). Literally.

Ezra and his team preached on the missional frontier to a people who could have easily deconstructed their faith. After all, the exile had been a shameful episode in their history, and now they were surrounded by enemies who wanted to retake the city. But the team of preachers embraced their missional moment. They proclaimed the truth of the Torah, established a pathway for the post-exilic good life, and fostered beauty amid the rubble of an ancient city.

Before we work to implement this approach in our contemporary preaching, we need to take a quick trip through church history to meet a legendary fourth-century North African preacher who followed in the footsteps of Ezra.

Augustine

Augustine was a bicultural preacher, shaped by both Africa and Rome.[6] He escaped childhood poverty to become an educated

---

[5] Makoto Fujimura, *Art + Faith: A Theology of Making* (Yale, 2020).

[6] Justo Gonzalez, *The Mestizo Augustine: A Theologian Between Two Cultures* (IVP, 2016).

professor of rhetoric.[7] As a teenager, he "walked the streets of Babylon" and infamously stole pears that he then wasted on pigs.[8] Augustine was converted when, upon hearing a child's voice say "Take up and read," he opened the Word of God and his doubt dissipated.[9] Augustine eventually became a minister of the gospel and served in both Africa and Europe.

The preeminent preacher wrote a classic text on pastoral ministry, usually called *On Christian Doctrine* (originally *De Doctrina Christiana*, in Latin). Toward the end of his treatise, he provided preachers with instruction on rhetoric. For Augustine, there were "three functions of eloquence: to teach, to delight, to sway."[10] In this ancient approach, we can see a focus on truth (teaching), goodness (swaying), and beauty (delighting).

Some preachers come off as robotic, merely reciting the truth that someone could have looked up on the internet. Other preachers seem to lose the truth of the text in their soaring rhetoric. Many preachers view this as an either/or situation, but not Augustine.

For Augustine, truth was paramount in preaching. The sermon's truth mattered more than its loveliness. Still, he thought there was value in learning to preach in various "modes." He

---

[7] Peter Brown, *Augustine of Hippo* (University of California Press, 1969), 21.

[8] Augustine, *The Confessions of St. Augustine,* trans. Edward Pusey (Washington Square Press, 1960), 23–24.

[9] Augustine, *Confessions*, 147–48.

[10] Augustine, *Teaching Christianity,* trans. Edmund Hill (New City Press, 1996), 222.

asserted, "It is the duty, therefore, of the eloquent churchman, when he is trying to persuade the people about something that has to be done, not only to teach, in order to instruct; not only to delight, in order to hold them; but also to sway, in order to conquer and win them."[11] Echoing Cicero, he said that preachers ought to be "listened to with understanding, with enjoyment, and with obedience."[12]

Augustine put this into practice when he preached a sermon in what is modern-day Algiers. He warned his listeners to resist the temptation to join the ongoing mob violence in the city. In describing this incident, he observed, "Still I did not consider I had achieved anything when I heard them applauding me, but only when I saw them weeping. Their applause only showed they were instructed and delighted, while their tears indicated that they were being swayed."[13]

The bicultural pastor was trained in the secular principles of ancient rhetoric. But he knew how to appropriate these techniques for preaching without placing his trust in them. His confidence, like Paul's, was in the gospel (Rom 1:16–17). That is why, amid his discussion on rhetoric, Augustine urged preachers to pray as part of their preparation.

For Augustine, it was important to interweave the triad of truth, goodness, and beauty into his sermons. He proclaimed the truth, persuaded his listeners to follow the path of goodness, and

---

[11] Augustine, *Teaching Christianity*, 224.

[12] Augustine, 227.

[13] Augustine, 241–42.

preached beautifully inspiring messages. Augustine was a both/and kind of preacher.

As an example, he once preached a sermon on Psalm 118 in Carthage, on the coast of Africa. He chose to devote his message to a phrase found in both the first and last verses of the song: "Give thanks to the LORD, for he is good." Much of the sermon was devoted to goodness, but it was goodness wed to truth and beauty. The preacher declared, "Nothing would be good unless it had been made by the good. And by what sort of good? By one that nobody made."[14]

The truth was foundational to the preacher's assertion. Augustine spoke of the created world, which was made and declared good by a perfectly good God. Furthermore, his wording, even translated from Latin, is elegant in its simplicity and beautiful in its brevity. In Augustine's sermon, form and function were woven together.

In another sermon, on Jesus's encounter with the violent storm (Matt 8:23–27), Augustine once again demonstrated a remarkable ability to embrace truth, goodness, and beauty. He sought to *sway*: "I want to urge you not to let the faith sleep in your hearts against the storms and waves of this world." He sought to *teach*: "It can scarcely be true that Christ the Lord had power over death, and did not have power over sleep, and that sleep possibly overtook the Almighty against his will, as he was out sailing." He sought to *delight* by trafficking in metaphor: "If the wind has driven us on

---

[14] Augustine, *Essential Sermons,* trans. Edmund Hill (New City, 2007), 50.

and shaken our souls with passion, don't let's despair; let's wake up Christ, and so sail on in a calm sea, and reach our home country."[15]

Since the Bible is true, we ought to confidently proclaim its message. Since the Bible is the pathway to human flourishing, we ought to model virtue and urge our listeners to embrace the good life. And since the Bible creates outposts of beauty in a darkened society, our sermons ought to be beautifully crafted messages that highlight the beauty of our God. Augustine excelled at all three tasks, because "The Christian gospel, for Augustine, wasn't just the answer to an intellectual question (though it was that); it was more like a shelter in a storm, a port for a wayward soul, nourishment for a prodigal who was famished."[16]

Retro Preaching for the Modern World

Louis Markos says that "the good, the true, and the beautiful are all action words that call us to take a quick glance backward and then trudge on with hope toward the distant land that is our true home."[17] How is this accomplished in the act of preaching? Preachers stand upon the missional frontier and glance toward the past, beckoning their listeners into the future. We do this as we embrace a retro style of preaching that imitates our spiritual ancestors (like Augustine) in proclaiming truth, modeling

---

[15] Augustine, *Essential Sermons*, 103–4.

[16] James K. A. Smith, *On the Road with Saint Augustine: A Real-World Spirituality for Restless Hearts* (Brazos, 2019), xii.

[17] Louis Markos, *Restoring Beauty: The Good, the True, and the Beautiful in the Writings of C. S. Lewis* (Biblica, 2010).

goodness, and fostering beauty. In the last section of this chapter, we will explore practical strategies for each element of the triad. We will start with the truth.

Proclaim the Truth

How do we proclaim truth in the modern world?

Preachers have a peculiar responsibility. We open an old book and then claim to speak for God. It's an audacious claim. Cult leaders, heretics, and terrorists have all made the same assertion. What makes us any different?

Preachers should only claim to speak for God if they are bearing witness to the truth of Scripture.[18] Even Paul's words were weighed by the Bereans (Acts 17:11). They wanted to know if what he said was true. The litmus test was simple: Did Paul's sermon correspond to the Bible? The Bereans judged Paul's sermon based on its truthfulness, according to the Old Testament Scriptures.

I live in a post-truth city. In Portland, the Bible is viewed with disdain (or more often, just ignored). It is not that spirituality cannot thrive here, because it does. Portland has been called one of the best places in the country to be a witch.[19] On a

---

[18] Sam Chan, *Preaching as the Word of God: Answering an Old Question with Speech-Act Theory* (Pickwick, 2016).

[19] See Camille Soleil, "Portland Is the Best Place in the Country to Be a Witch," *Willamette Week*, February 12, 2020, https://www.wweek.com/culture/2020/02/12/portland-is-the-best-place-in-the-country-to-be-a-witch/.

rainy spring day, you can even stumble into the faerie dance of an emerging neo-pagan Druid movement.[20]

Our neighbors are incurably spiritual. The apostle Paul would no doubt note that they are "extremely religious" (Acts 17:22). But in their dizzying array of remixed spiritualities, Portlandites believe that truth (if it is real) is personally discovered.[21] Into that scene steps the preacher, who claims to have a message from another world.

The religious scene that Jesus encountered was a bit different, but with competing rabbinic schools with different scribes, different rabbis, and different interpretations of the Torah. But when Jesus preached his masterful "Sermon on the Mount," it landed like a rocket. "The crowds were astonished at his teaching, because he was teaching them like one who had authority, and not like their scribes" (Matt 7:28–29).

The scribes appealed to the authority of another. Jesus spoke for himself. The Son of God was his own final authority. When we preach, we don't have that same kind of internal authority. Yet our preaching can still exude a sense of authority. How is that possible?

It is possible, first, when we declare "This is what the Lord says" (see Isa 48:17). Missional preaching is not an invitation

---

[20] See Melissa Binder, "Pagans Find Belonging in Blossoming Congregation," *Oregon Live/The Oregonian*, May 1, 2016, https://www.oregonlive.com/faith/2016/05/may_day_beltane_adf.html.

[21] Tara Isabella Burton coined the phrase "Religiously Remixed": Tara Isabella Burton, *Strange Rites: New Religions for a Godless World* (Public Affairs, 2020).

to ditch the script of Scripture. Rather, it is a commission to embrace the Bible more deeply and proclaim its truths in the chaotic context of modern culture. When we proclaim the Word of God, our preaching is infused with heavenly authority. That means that it is on us to make sure we are speaking for God, and not for ourselves, or for another. This is why careful exegesis of Scripture is so vital. This is why we study diligently so that we can correctly teach the truth (2 Tim 2:15). There can be no shortcuts in sermon preparation, especially on the frontier of unbelief.

Second, it is possible for our sermons to exude authority when we believe what we preach. I have heard dull, lifeless sermons in which the preacher recited textual truths. I have also heard sermons when the preacher was so gripped by the glory of God that he seemed like a messenger from another world. This moment of truth on fire occurs when we actually believe the message. Is gospel proclamation your job or joy, your duty or delight? Preachers preach because we must. We have been captivated by the goodness of God, and we must speak about it. When we do, we preach with authority. And in a world awash with disinformation, our neighbors need to hear a calm, confident assertion of truth.

Third, our preaching exudes authority when our real life matches our rhetoric. Do our deeds on a Thursday correspond to our words on a Sunday? On the missional frontier, everyone is viewed with suspicion. People are cynical, especially about religious leaders. If we are going to speak for God, we must demonstrate that we are living for him. As we discussed in the second chapter, authenticity is crucial when preaching to those who do not yet believe. Jesus modeled authenticity when he spoke like no other, and then lived like no other.

When we say what God said, believe what we say, and live out what we say, we can speak with authority on the frontier of unbelief. And when we do, we will be signposts pointing toward the One who is the truth.

Celebrate Goodness

Our sermons should also celebrate goodness. Humans hunger for the good life. In New York, there is a clear and compelling version of the good life. People move to New York to pursue their dreams. Wall Street represents one version of that dream, a possible fulfillment of the good life. We are told, "Come to New York and get rich." The film industry represents another iteration of the good life. Occasionally I've seen signs plastered all over a particular block, warning people to move their cars because a show or movie was shooting there that week. That created excitement: Would we catch a glimpse of a star? Lots of New Yorkers were hoping to be "discovered" and land the role of a lifetime.

In every culture, in every era, people want to flourish. They crave the good life. When we preach on the frontier of unbelief, we have an opportunity to demonstrate that the Bible is the only sure path to the good life, and that goodness can only be defined counterculturally.

The French mathematician Blaise Pascal is famous for his philosophical musings on Christianity. As a Christian, he declared, "Men despise religion. They hate it and are afraid it may be true. The cure for this is first to show that religion is not contrary to reason, but worthy of reverence and respect. Next make it attractive, make good men wish it were true, and then show that it is."[22]

Pascal understood that sometimes we cannot start with the question of truth. We must start with the question of goodness and work our way toward truth. The mathematician-philosopher believed that Christianity "promises the true good."[23] On the frontier of unbelief, our listeners desire goodness, but they have a warped perspective on goodness. Our task, as missional preachers, is to demonstrate that the Bible is the true pathway to human flourishing.

We do this first by focusing on Jesus: no one has ever been more authentically human. In showing us what it means to be human, Jesus painted a picture of the good life. Ironically, the virtues that Jesus proclaimed and embodied have had a mixed reception in the modern world. Love? Yes. Chastity? Definitely not!

Modern humans love Jesus, as long as they can keep him contained. Yet Jesus refuses our efforts at domestication. He spoke of the good life (his Sermon on the Mount is a road map) and he embodied the good life (all four Gospels narrate the story of a man who lived a remarkably different life). If we are to follow Pascal's lead, we must demonstrate that Christianity offers up a pathway to goodness. That path begins and ends with Jesus. Our

---

[22] Blaise Pascal, *Pensées*, trans. A. J. Krailsheimer (Penguin, 1972), 34.

[23] Blaise Pascal, *The Pensées and the Provincial Letters* (Random House, 1941), 64.

listeners on the missional frontier are searching for a good life. We must demonstrate that what they have really been searching for all along is a Good Person.

We can also celebrate goodness in our missional sermons by consistently teaching the virtues espoused in the Bible. The Beatitudes and the fruit of the Spirit are never out of style in the kingdom of heaven. If we are going to invite people on a pilgrimage to the City of God, we must make clear what is involved. Oftentimes this will mean a countercultural proclamation of biblical goodness.

When we teach on goodness, we must ground it in the creation of the cosmos. Repeatedly in Genesis we are told that God made a good world. Why does Moses want us to know this? In part because he wants us to know that God is good. The universe is good because it was made by a good God. That also means that the law of God is good because it is written by a good God.

Our listeners may not be convinced that there is a real Creator who made a good world. But, as Pascal noted, we have an opportunity to persuade our skeptics in a roundabout way. We can paint a compelling picture of the good life, one focused on Jesus, on countercultural virtues, and on the design of creation. And as we do, we pray that the Holy Spirit will awaken in our listeners a desire for the Bible to be true.

On the frontier of unbelief, goodness is almost always cherished more than truth. That is why it often makes sense to follow Pascal's lead and begin with goodness. As we tap into the universal desire for the good life, we have a chance to demonstrate that Christianity is both good and true.

Celebrate Beauty

Finally, our sermons ought to celebrate beauty. First, our sermons ought to be as beautiful as possible. As Augustine would remind us, form and function belong together. And surprisingly enough, we can delight skeptical listeners with a well-crafted sermon. In our church plant in Brooklyn, I preached to people who understood the power of words, including an opera singer, an English professor, and a writer for a web series. How I said something mattered almost as much as what I said.

This is a call for preachers to hone their craft: to refuse the temptation to get sloppy or to phone it in. After our exegetical work is done, our rhetorical work begins. And that work is crucial. We are telling the best story that has ever been written. Why would we use boring language to retell it? We are describing the resplendent King of the cosmos. Why would we settle for uninspiring speech? When we preach on the frontier of unbelief, we have a chance to dazzle non-Christians with the person and work of Jesus. We have a chance to enchant non-Christians with a vision of the triune God. We must not let that opportunity slip between our fingers.

Second, our sermons ought to foster beauty in our neighborhoods. The words of our sermons do not vanish into a void. They do something. And when they are tethered to Scripture, they do what Scripture does (Isa 55:11). When our words escape our lips and travel through the air, they are heard by listeners who may choose to react in a myriad of ways. They might pray, contemplate, obey, or reject (to name a few possible responses). We are hoping that the Spirit will use our utterances to do something beautiful in our local contexts. And the possibilities are endless.

In a society dominated by darkness and despair, beauty is a lifeline. Our sermons ought to be life-giving artifacts of loveliness, which foster beauty amid the rubble of society. If our neighborhoods are dark, our sermons should spark light. If our cities are diseased, our sermons should heal. If our homes are despairing, our sermons should create hope. If our society is decaying, our sermons should foster beauty.

Paradoxically, preaching that fosters beauty will be cruciform. Two thousand years later, we are still haunted by the blood-stained reality of the old rugged cross. And yet, what could be more lovely? Cross-shaped preaching subverts the cultural standards of beauty by holding up the cross as the supreme example of beauty. And it will force us to reckon with the fact that Jesus came and identified with the poor and the powerless, with tax collectors and prostitutes. Preaching that fosters beauty will not create tidy enclaves of the righteous. Instead, it will cultivate messy communities where God is at work and his grace runs rampant. Having experienced this, I can testify that this is a thing of beauty to behold.

God is true, good, and beautiful, and the book he inspired provides abundant evidence of this triad. The Bible is the true story of the world. It is the pathway to human flourishing (the good life). And it creates outposts of beauty amid the rubble of our world. On the frontier of unbelief, our sermons should proclaim truth, model goodness, and generate beauty.

Good preaching stimulates the mind, stokes the conscience, and stirs the imagination. That is the style of preaching that will gain an audience on the missional frontier, even if the sermons are about the puzzling book of Ecclesiastes.

6

Preach Jesus

"Why is Jesus so kind?" My new friend asked a simple, yet profound question after listening to one of my sermons on Galatians. Having just relocated from China to Portland, my friend was attending the English worship service of the church I currently serve. When he first arrived, he told me that he and his wife were there to learn English and learn about God.

A few weeks later, his straightforward question startled me. Not because I disagreed with the premise; of course, I believe that Jesus is kind. But what struck me about the question is that this was someone's first impression of Jesus. Sometimes those of us who have spent decades in the church can forget what it is like to encounter Jesus for the first time. For my new friend, Jesus did not seem like a theological abstraction to be debated. Instead, he seemed like a person with a surprising depth of compassion.

I was grateful for the question, and I responded by pointing out that Jesus is so kind because Jesus is God, and God is love. Then my newfound friend told me that our congregation had treated him and his wife with kindness (always encouraging for a pastor to hear). I told him that we were able to extend kindness because we had been transformed by God. I shared the gospel with him, centering the conversation on the amazing kindness of God, manifested at the cross. My friend remarked: "I need to think about this."

He was gone the next Sunday. Ministry to international people embraces the tension of transience. Migrants are on the move, looking for jobs, for family, and for connection. After our conversation about the kindness of Jesus, my friend and his wife departed for Los Angeles, seeking employment. Over the course of several months, we texted off and on about the kindness of Jesus. Incredibly, my friend recently told me via text that he had decided to follow Jesus and had been baptized! He finally understood that Jesus loves him and that he proved it at the cross (Rom 5:8). The kindness of God led him to repentance (Rom 2:4).

On the frontier of unbelief, the central question to be answered is the one posed by Jesus two millennia ago: "Who do you say that I am?" (Matt 16:15). Our secular neighbors must figure out what to make of Jesus. Our deconstructing churchgoers must decide what to do with Jesus, and our pluralistic friends must decide who they think he is. This is why, when we launched our Brooklyn church plant, we started in a Jamaican restaurant, with a six-week evangelistic Bible study called "Who is Jesus and why should I care?"

Who is Jesus, and why should I care? It's *the* question that missional preaching must answer. Our listeners might find elements of Christianity compelling. They might appreciate our concern for the poor, our construction of hospitals, and our involvement in the abolition of slavery. But who is Jesus? That question trumps everything else, and it demands an answer.

That is why, when members of other religious traditions knock on our door to evangelize us, I don't spend much time focusing on what we share in common (though there is some overlap in what we believe). Instead, I make a beeline to Jesus. I want the conversation to center on him, because he is the sun around which all our religious beliefs orbit. Those who knock on my door to proselytize me might not agree with me about Jesus. But having a conversation about him is the most important service I can offer to them. And when we preach on the missional frontier, having a conversation about Jesus is the best service we can offer to those who doubt or disbelieve.

Missionary Lesslie Newbigin understood this spiritual need and asserted, "We have to preach Christ. That is really our only business in the pulpit."[1] Preachers can become distracted by many topics (we will discuss that temptation later in the chapter). Yet they must always major on the majors and center their sermons on Christ. The most fruitful sermons in a missionary encounter are always those that exalt Jesus. But to do this well, we have to take a quick detour to discuss methods of preaching Christ.

---

[1] Lesslie Newbigin, *The Good Shepherd: Meditations on Christian Ministry in Today's World* (Eerdmans, 1977), 24.

In chapter 4 we explored how to preach the Bible as the true story of the world. I briefly mentioned that biblical theology is a useful discipline because it helps us to discover how the Bible tells one story, and how its various parts fit together. In this chapter, we must discern the most appropriate way to preach Jesus from all of Scripture. If exalting Jesus is the goal of our missional sermons, and we preach from a biblical text that does not mention Jesus (probably one from the Old Testament), how do we accomplish our mission?

As far as I know, all evangelicals believe that we should preach Jesus. But how we do that is debated. Some prefer allegorical approaches to reading the Bible, ones that end up discerning (or sometimes, "discovering") Jesus in biblical imagery.[2] Others see every text as a building block in our spiritual formation, one culminating in our Christlikeness.[3] Others believe that Christ is the truest fulfillment of each narrative of Scripture.[4]

In my opinion, each of these approaches has some merit. They are all attempts to take seriously the words of Christ: "Beginning with Moses and all the Prophets, he interpreted for them the things concerning himself in all the Scriptures" (Luke 24:27).

---

[2] This approach was favored by some of the Church Fathers.

[3] This approach, termed "Christiconic Preaching," is championed by Abraham Kuruvilla, *A Manual for Preaching: The Journey from Text to Sermon* (Baker, 2019).

[4] One of the primary advocates of Christ-centered preaching was the late Timothy Keller, *Preaching: Communicating Faith in an Age of Skepticism* (Penguin, 2015).

On the road to Emmaus, Jesus taught across the Old Testament, demonstrating that it all pointed to him.

I prefer the approach of my colleague, Steve Mathewson, who argues that Jesus is the goal of the entire Bible. The storyline of Scripture moves us toward Jesus. Every narrative, every prophecy, and every poem serve to advance the narrative agenda of Scripture and bring us closer to Jesus.[5] And yet each individual piece of biblical literature must be treated on its own terms. Christopher Wright notes the Old Testament is like a long bus ride that takes us to the destination: "The Old Testament tells the story that Jesus completes."[6] Those who preach on the frontier of unbelief will need to grapple with how best to preach Jesus from *all* of Scripture. We must take seriously each unit of text (the trees) as well as the overarching story that is told (the forest). When we miss neither the forest nor the trees, we arrive at Jesus the Messiah—the key to missional preaching.

In a sermon series on Judges, I came to a unique passage about idolatry in ancient Israel (see Judges 17–18). The writer recounts how a Levite became the private priest of the warmongering tribe of Dan. The spiritual leader used sacred rhetoric and practices to ensure the favor of Yahweh. In doing so, he was following the lead of his neighbors throughout the ancient Near Eastern world.

---

[5] This is called Christotelic Preaching. See Steven Mathewson, *The Art of Preaching Old Testament Narrative* (Baker, 2021), 15–26.

[6] Christopher J. H. Wright, *How to Preach and Teach the Old Testament for All Its Worth* (Zondervan, 2016), 27.

It was common in that era for people to manipulate the gods. If you wanted them to bless your crops, you offered a sacrifice. If you wanted a fertile womb, you offered a sacrifice. If you wanted victory in battle, you offered a sacrifice. People believed that the gods could be manipulated into doing the bidding of those who offer up the right performance.

But Yahweh was not like that. He could not be appeased through performance, because Israel always fell short (in fact, we all do; Rom 3:23). After explaining the details of the text, and discussing our propensity to succumb to idolatry, I talked about grace. I highlighted the tendency of the characters in the text to think that God could be manipulated through our effort. And I explained that grace is the theme of the Bible. Many years after the Judges, Jesus would come to offer us a gift. He cannot be manipulated since we cannot perform at a level that would earn his love. But he dispenses it freely because he is good.

At the conclusion of my sermon, someone who was not a Christian approached me with tears in her eyes. She said that she had never fully understood grace before. All it took was a strange story from the book of Judges! This is what missional preaching does. It honestly deals with the details of any text and points people to the goal of that text: Jesus. As I said in the introduction, *missional preaching engages people at the frontier of unbelief and invites them to take a journey toward Jesus.* When we do this, we are standing on the shoulders of giants. In this chapter, we will consider two of them.

John the Baptist

John the Baptist was one strange preacher (Mark 1:4–8). For starters, his church was the wilderness; he preached under the open sky. Then there was his outfit. He did not wear a clerical collar, robe, suit, or even skinny jeans. This preacher wore a camel-hair garment that probably reminded people of Elijah. His message was stark: "Repent, because the kingdom of heaven has come near!" (Matt 3:2). People traveled to the wilderness to hear this odd preacher deliver stern messages. When they heard him, many were convicted and baptized in the Jordan River, confessing their sins.

When John the Baptist preached, people listened. Maybe it was his location, maybe it was his outfit, maybe it was his diet. Most likely, it was the announcement that he delivered: The long-awaited kingdom of God was at hand. This was good news for the people of Israel, who had prayed for this moment for millennia.

John's preaching, however, was not all warm and fuzzy. It was certainly good news, but his message seemed to be designed to ruffle some feathers. When the Pharisees and Sadducees came to a baptismal service, he rebuked them. He called them a "brood of vipers" and warned them to produce fruit consistent with repentance. It was not enough for Israel's religious leaders to immerse themselves in water. A public confession was not sufficient; John wanted to see life change. John warned that someone was coming who would separate the chaff from the wheat, burning the chaff in a fire that would never go out. John the Baptist preached good news, mixed with a dose of judgment (Matt 3:7–12).

John the Baptist was not just any preacher. He was the forerunner. Long ago, Malachi had predicted that Elijah would return "before the great and terrible day of the Lord" (Mal 4:5). When Gabriel announced that John would be born, he told John's father that John would go before the Lord in the spirit and power of Elijah. He would prepare the people for the Lord (Luke 1:16–17).

But it was not merely prophecy that linked John to Jesus. They were also family. John and Jesus were relatives who met before they were even born. When Elizabeth was in her final trimester of pregnancy, she received a visit from Mary (who, though still a virgin, miraculously carried Jesus in her womb). When Mary stepped into the room, Elizabeth sensed that she was in the presence of greatness (Luke 1:39–45).

Elizabeth explained to Mary that when she first heard Mary's voice, the child within her leaped for joy. The unborn preacher was elated to be in the presence of the unborn Messiah. Even as an unborn baby, John the Baptist had a connection to Jesus. He would be born before Jesus by about six months. John came first because his job was to prepare the way. His job was to preach Jesus.

Years later, Jesus oversaw baptisms in the Judean countryside. The Bible does not tell us much about these baptisms. However, we do know that they attracted quite a bit of attention. In fact, the baptisms unsettled the disciples of John the Baptist. They protested to John: "Rabbi, the one you testified about, and who was with you across the Jordan, is baptizing—and everyone is going to him" (John 3:26).

Apparently, the disciples of John were envious because there was now another game in town. Previously, their teacher had all the attention to himself. People had come to the wilderness to see him, to hear his message, and to be baptized. Now, many were turning to Jesus. John was unfazed. He reminded his disciples of his message. John had never claimed to be the Messiah, only his forerunner (John 3:28). The herald's job was simply to make way for the King.

John likened it to the role of a best man at a wedding (John 3:29). The best man doesn't steal the show and marry the bride. John essentially declared: "I'm the best man. My job is to make sure that the bride marries Jesus." And then he delivered his now-famous line: "He must increase, but I must decrease" (v. 30).

John knew how to run in his lane. His role was to prepare the way for the Messiah. Now that the Messiah had arrived, John could fade into the background. The Baptizer knew his mission was to preach Jesus. No amount of personal ambition would interfere with that task. In fact, people would later point out that John performed no signs and wonders. Unlike Elijah, he merely testified about the Messiah. And everything he said about Jesus was true (John 10:40–42).

Perhaps it was this singular focus on his vocation that prompted Jesus to praise John the Baptist. He declared, "Among those born of women no one greater than John the Baptist has appeared. . . . If you're willing to accept it, he is the Elijah who is to come" (Matt 11:11, 14).

John the Baptist operated on the frontier of unbelief, preparing the hearts of his fellow Israelites for the arrival of the King. He preached Jesus, from beginning to end.

But this devoted approach to preaching Jesus does not mean that John never preached on anything else. Sometimes people mistakenly believe that orienting our sermons around Jesus means that we never talk about the details of a text or exhort our listeners to obey the ethical commands of Scripture. John certainly preached Jesus, but he was also able to multitask.

The forerunner of the King also found the time to preach against a false king called Herod, who was merely a puppet of Rome. In a land in which people theoretically observed the law of God, it was disturbing to see Herod Antipas take his brother's wife for himself. Her name was Herodias, and John the Baptist could not remain silent. He told Herod, "It is not lawful for you to have your brother's wife" (Mark 6:18). This prophetic preaching cost John his head (vv. 14–29).

John preached against sin and exhorted an impostor to submit to the demands of the Law. Preaching that has Christ as its goal flows out of every text and trickles out into all of life. That is because Jesus is the true King—the King of all of life. Preaching Jesus means emphasizing his words, his life, and his saving work. It involves an all-of-Scripture approach that seeks to submit to the Sovereign of the universe.

At the end of his life, the Baptizer had a moment of doubt. Imprisoned for his courageous sermonizing, he dispatched messengers to Jesus. They asked, on behalf of John, "Are you the one who is to come, or should we expect someone else?" (Matt 11:2–3). Jesus responded: "Go and report to John what you hear and see: The blind receive their sight, the lame walk, those with leprosy are cleansed, the deaf hear, the dead are raised, and the poor are told the good news, and blessed is the one who isn't offended by me" (Matt 11:4–6).

John's momentary doubt is a timely reminder for those of us who preach in the late-modern age. Even staunchly committed Christians might be on the edge of losing their faith—on the verge of deconstructing. Jesus did not berate John for his doubt. He understood that you can believe and disbelieve at the same time (Mark 9:24).

Instead of chastising his cousin, Jesus simply pointed out what the Messiah had done. People had been healed, resurrections had occurred, and the poor had heard the good news. Jesus identified those signs that were occurring because the Messiah was active in the world. The Son of God responded to doubt by pointing to himself.

Preaching Jesus is a nonnegotiable task of Christian preaching, especially when we operate on the frontier of unbelief. Like John, we have the privilege of introducing our neighbors to the King, because he is good for their souls. And like John, we will discover when we preach Jesus that he is good for our souls too.

S. M. Lockridge

Shadrach Meshach (S. M.) Lockridge was a twentieth-century Baptist pastor and a professor of preaching. The African American pastor served a Baptist congregation in San Diego for forty years. But he did not stop there. Lockridge was involved in the civil rights movement. He was also a committed evangelist, preaching in forty-four countries and on twenty-one air force bases.[7] He was a gifted preacher of the gospel. Of Lockridge's many gifts in the pulpit, his primary strength was pointing people to Jesus. Some of his sermons have become legendary for just that reason. We will consider two.

In his sermon "Amen," Lockridge ended with a doxological crescendo that has come to be called "That's My King!" In church circles, if you say, "That's my King," some folks will still think of the five-minute climax to Lockridge's famous sermon, in which the preacher introduced Jesus as his "seven-way King." The hour-long sermon includes these famous lines:

> My King is the key to knowledge. He's the wellspring of wisdom. He's the doorway of deliverance. He's the pathway of peace. He's the roadway of righteousness. He's the highway of holiness. He's the gateway of glory. . . . Do you know him?[8]

Reverend Lockridge preached this sermon in a variety of locations. I highly encourage you to listen to a recording of it. One such recording can be found on the Moody Audio website, at https://moodyaudio.com/products/amen-0. It will thrill your soul if you will take the time to hear the passion with which Lockridge exalted Christ. He was consumed with the glory of

---

[7] See Carl J. Bradford, "Shadrach Meshach (S.M.) Lockridge: Pastor and Evangelist," in *A History of Evangelism in North America*, ed. Thomas P. Johnston (Kregel, 2021), 219–21. See also https://www.youtube.com/watch?v=Oil68-DmFJo.

[8] S. M. Lockridge, "Amen," 1970s sermon, transcribed from Moody Audio, https://moodyaudio.com/products/amen-0.

God. John the Baptist would have been proud because S. M. Lockridge preached Jesus. He lifted a finger and pointed people toward the Son of God.

In another sermon, Lockridge spoke eloquently about the horror and grief of Good Friday. His repeated refrain was unforgettable: "It's Friday, but Sunday's comin'."[9] With the skills of a seasoned storyteller, Lockridge walked his listeners through the emotional toll of Good Friday. He declared, "It's Friday. The world's winning. People are sinning. And evil's grinning." Listeners are swept into the biblical story and can identify with the motifs of despair and defeat.

But Lockridge was not finished because Jesus was not finished. He announced, "It's Friday. But let me tell you something. Sunday's comin'." The evangelistic preacher knew that most people identify with the darkness of Good Friday and the silence of Holy Saturday. After all, even though Christians have already been raised with Christ, we await the fullness of our resurrection.

Lockridge continued: "It's Friday. The earth trembles. The sky grows dark. My King yields his spirit. It's Friday. Hope is lost. Death has won. Sin has conquered and Satan's just a laughin'. It's Friday. Jesus is buried. A soldier stands guard. And a rock is rolled into place. But it's Friday. It is only Friday. Sunday is a comin'!" With short, staccato phrases, and masterful

---

[9] Audio of the sermon excerpt was uploaded to YouTube in 2000 by Carpenter Missions and can be found here: https://www.youtube.com/watch?v=QS2wPotScZY. The transcript used as the basis of this section can be found at Justin Taylor, "It's Friday—but Sunday's Comin'," *TGC Blogs*, April 18, 2014: https://www.thegospelcoalition.org/blogs/justin-taylor/its-fridaybut-sundays-comin/.

use of repetition, Lockridge acknowledged the grim reality of the moment but also beckoned hopefully to the future. Easter was just around the corner. Jesus was about to break the bars of Hades.

For S. M. Lockridge, preaching Jesus was an art form. Everyday preachers like us might never measure up to his soaring rhetoric. But I think Lockridge would tell us, "Just preach Jesus. He's enough."

Preaching Jesus in the Wilderness

Like John the Baptist, we preach in the wilderness. Ours is a wilderness of unbelief, characterized by idolatry and doubt. Like John, we probably seem a little odd to our listeners. But also like John, we have a responsibility to preach Jesus. In this final section, we will briefly explore how to go about preaching Jesus in a pluralistic wasteland.

First, we must proclaim the gospel. Worshipping idols can be comfortable because they never talk back. But in a world awash with idols, Jesus refuses to go quietly into the night. Preachers dare to speak for God in the missionary encounter between the gospel and culture. This means that we preach Jesus, the One God who speaks to humanity. If we are going to bear witness in a world characterized by idolatry, then we must learn how to preach Jesus. That starts with the good news.

The cross is a necessity for Christian preachers. Paul understood this, and declared, "For the word of the cross is foolishness to those who are perishing, but it is the power of God to us who are being saved. . . . For the Jews ask for signs and the Greeks seek wisdom, but we preach Christ crucified" (1 Cor 1:18, 22–23). Paul was not against the use of oratory in the pulpit. His letters show clear traces of rhetorical artistry. Instead, Paul was saying that fancy words that lack the crucial content of the cross are devoid of power.

Ben Witherington notes, "In contrast to both Jews and Gentiles, Paul preaches the paradoxical notion of a crucified God."[10] Mysteriously, only the crucified Creator of the cosmos could become the power of God to the Romans and the wisdom of God to the Jews. For millennia, preachers have followed in Paul's footsteps by emphasizing the cross.

We do so because only the cross unmasks our idols and interrogates our questions. It unmasks our idols by demonstrating what we unwittingly worship. Humans were made to worship God. But as we live east of Eden, we tend to worship the creation instead of the Creator, fashioning gods in our own image. The Greeks worshipped wisdom and the Jews idolized signs. And so, God revealed himself as a crucified Messiah, the ultimate power and wisdom of God.

Our idols don't always look like statues on a shrine. They usually hide in plain sight because we don't think of them as idols. But the scandal of the cross upends everything we know. It reveals our values, and too often they do not reflect the kingdom of God. The cross of Christ pulls the mask off our idols and points out the absurdity of our false worship.

---

[10] Ben Witherington III, *Conflict and Community in Corinth: A Socio-Rhetorical Commentary on 1 and 2 Corinthians* (Eerdmans, 1995), 113.

We also preach Christ crucified because the cross interrogates our questions. Golgotha's bloodstained cross is countercultural. It reminds us (as it reminded the Jews and the Greeks whom Paul addressed at Corinth) that our questions are sometimes misguided. Sometimes the questions we are asking of God aren't even the right questions. We can be a lot like the wandering Israelites, who wondered how God was going to fill their bellies. Satisfying hunger is instinctual, but Jesus touches both body and soul. His plan is to give us an entirely new kind of life—eternal life (John 17:3). When we gaze upon the horrific beauty of the cross, we see a God who made himself weak and vulnerable for us. When we understand the cross, many of our questions fade away. We are given a new grammar so that we can begin to ask the questions we should have been asking all along.

The old rugged cross is more than a cherished hymn. It is more than a symbol. It is the altar upon which the Son of God paid for our sins and the place in which we died with Christ (Gal 2:20). That haunting hill of Calvary was and is a crucible, the place where we realize we are not masters of our universe; we are broken wanderers who stumble through life. The Place of the Skull reminds us, again and again, that we are loved by a crucified King.

Preaching Jesus demands an almost relentless focus on the cross. That is why Paul determined to preach Christ crucified. We must do the same.

Second, we must preach the authentic Jesus. Let's face it: We see a lot of confusion about who Jesus is. If you poll your neighbors, you might get a variety of answers. For some, Jesus was a religious guru who dished out pithy words of wisdom. For some, Jesus was a revolutionary who relished a confrontation with the powers that be. Some of our neighbors even believe that Jesus was a prophet who paved the way for another. People have been trying to ascertain the identity of Christ for two millennia. That's why Jesus asked the disciples, "Who do you say that I am?" (Matt 16:15).

Given all the confusion about Jesus, it is essential to preach the authentic Jesus. One way I tried to do that in Brooklyn was by preaching a series called I AM: Jesus in His Own Words. It was primarily a study of the seven "I AM" statements of Jesus in John's Gospel. I told our congregation (which, as I've noted, was regularly populated by skeptics) that it was important to hear directly from Jesus. We've heard what other people think about him, and who they say he is. But what did he say about himself? Who did the Son of Man claim to be?

When we explored that Jesus was, among other things, the Light of the World, the Bread of Life, and the Door, it opened new opportunities to come face-to-face with the Pioneer of our faith (Heb 12:2). People must understand who Jesus is before making a decision. It must, however, be on Jesus's terms. We must accept his own testimony and take him as he is. Missional preachers need to continually bring their listeners back to Jesus. Those who live on the frontier of unbelief need repeated opportunities to encounter the transformative man from Nazareth.

Third, we must resist the temptation to preach on the wrong things. It can be difficult for a preacher to stay on message. We have a chance to deliver a monologue, and we get to choose the content. And sometimes we veer off course. We end up focusing on things that are of lesser importance.

Sometimes this means that we make our sermons into extended discussions about how to be "better" at something: a better husband, wife, parent, single, employee, employer, citizen, student, etc. Now, the Word of God certainly makes us better human beings. How could it not? It is living and active and incredibly powerful. But the Scriptures are not a road map to happy living in this era or in any other. As we discussed in chapter 3, the Bible is the true story of the world. When we make our sermons about how we can improve ourselves, we end up accidentally taking the focus off of Jesus. The Bible points to him, not us.

Preachers can also preach about the wrong things by emphasizing political and cultural issues in the pulpit. We live in a time of deep polarization in which everything is viewed through a political lens. People in our churches are bombarded with political messages every day. As a result, the people in the pews are thinking about politics more often than they should. One of the ways a preacher can serve them is by reminding them of what is ultimate.

When a congregation is flustered because of something happening in Washington, they need to see a preacher who is not frantic, and who calmly explains the text, preaching Jesus above all else. And this is especially vital on the missional frontier. People appear to be migrating away from evangelical churches, in part because they are fed up with excessive politicization.[11] Culture wars create compelling electoral strategies, but they do not generate persuasive sermons. When the streets are on fire, preach Jesus. When Congress is in chaos, preach Jesus. When "the other side" is coming for our children, preach Jesus.

Now, I will be the first to admit that this is a difficult line to walk, and I am not sure I have always gotten it just right. After all, preaching about the risen Lord invariably brings us into confrontation with the idols of our age. Remember John, who pointed to Jesus? He also managed to preach against the injustice of a political leader who violated God's design for sexuality. John's preaching cost him his head.

Over time, I have preached on cultural issues that are deemed political in today's climate. I have discussed abortion, marriage, gender dysphoria, immigration, racial justice, the environment, nationalism, and violence. But I try to let the text drive the conversation (after all, we are preaching, not giving speeches). When you are preaching through a book of the Bible, you are forced to preach what is right in front of you, and that can be a lifesaving exercise in self-control for the preacher.

What is more, it signals to the skeptic on the missional frontier that you are not simply a partisan for a sociopolitical agenda. You have a higher calling: to steward the gospel—to preach Jesus. And yes, preaching Jesus will sometimes lead us

---

[11] Russell Moore, *Losing Our Religion: An Altar Call for Evangelical America* (Sentinel, 2023), 36–38.

into deep waters as we teach people everything that Jesus commanded. But the person with fragile faith who listens to our sermons does not need a panicked speech about what is wrong with society. She needs hope for her soul. She needs good news. She needs Jesus.

When I pastored in Brooklyn, we devoted a series to the book of Colossians, and we called it "A Theory of Everything." Because that's how Paul viewed Jesus. He is the One in whom God's fulness dwells. I think it is fitting to end this chapter with a glorious first-century hymn, from Colossians. Let us preach this Jesus!

> He is the image of the invisible God,
> the firstborn over all creation.
> For everything was created by him,
> in heaven and on earth,
> the visible and the invisible,
> whether thrones or dominions
> or rulers or authorities—
> all things have been created through him and for him.
> He is before all things,
> and by him all things hold together.
> He is also the head of the body, the church;
> he is the beginning,
> the firstborn from the dead,
> so that he might come to have
> first place in everything.
> For God was pleased to have

all his fullness dwell in him,
and through him to reconcile
everything to himself,
whether things on earth or things in heaven,
by making peace
through his blood, shed on the cross.[12]

[12] Col 1:15–20. For a contemporary expression of the truths of this ancient poem, listen to Shai Linne's song "Lord of All": https://www.youtube.com/watch?v=tYmiZaGOlTs.

CONCLUSION

Change is inevitable; it is like a freight train barreling down the tracks. My wife and I have four kids. While writing this, our youngest just turned three, our oldest will turn eleven, and I will turn forty! What happened? Where did the time go? Can't everything just stay the same? Some of that nostalgia is a natural part of human life as we confront the certainty of change. Other changes, however, appear more threatening than the consistent march of time.

Secularism is on the rise (at least in the West). Pluralism is here to stay (and so are our neighbors who belong to various religions). And deconstruction is the topic du jour that rattles the church as the faith of the faithful fades. But now is not the time to panic. In a post-Easter world, the sky is not falling, and it never will.

The late Timothy Keller was right when he urged, "Instead of wringing our hands over the loss of cultural influence in Western culture, this decline should prompt us to examine ourselves, pray, and work toward a new missionary engagement with Western culture."[1] Our fresh missionary encounter with America will involve a variety of strategies. But one of those strategies must be preaching.

That is because God has ordained the preaching of his Word as the means by which our neighbors hear and respond to the gospel. As Paul said, "How can they hear without a preacher?" (Rom 10:14). That was true in the first century and it's still true today. Amid all the changes that surround us, the gospel hasn't changed. It's still good news for:

addicts
artists
immigrants
Republicans
Democrats
the abused
the poor
racists
victims
Pharisees
me

As the frontier of unbelief envelops us, we must resist the temptations of flight and fight. Instead, we must stick it out on the missional frontier, patiently proclaiming the good news. I

[1] Timothy Keller, *How to Reach the West Again* (Redeemer City to City, 2020), 4.

hope you can use some of the strategies in this book. Perhaps you can grow in watching your tone, in acknowledging the elephant in the room, and in narrating the true story of the world. Perhaps you will be ready to answer; you will celebrate truth, goodness, and beauty; and you will faithfully preach Jesus. Maybe you will even improvise some of your own strategies. Along the way, you will probably make some missteps in your preaching. I do. After all, we are only human.

But we can take great comfort in the fact that Jesus precedes us on the journey. I agree with Newbigin, who said, "I think that the deepest motive for mission is simply the desire to be with Jesus where he is, on the frontier between the reign of God and the usurped dominion of the devil."[2] As you dare to speak for God on the frontier of unbelief, you will find joy in knowing that Jesus stands with you and speaks through you. That is good news for preachers.

[2] Lesslie Newbigin, *A Word in Season: Perspectives on Christian World Missions* (Eerdmans, 1994), 129.

ACKNOWLEDGMENTS

Writing a book is a community project. Over the last few years, I have had the privilege of teaching homiletics at Western Seminary. I am grateful to Dean Mathews and to President Conniry for giving me the opportunity to explore these concepts in the classroom. In the process, I have discovered that my students at Western are world-class. They have allowed me to field-test new ideas for communicating the gospel in an age of unbelief. This book is better because of them.

I am also indebted to those who generously read the manuscript and provided valuable critique: Taylor Field, Manuel Sosa, Ken Yeo, Ron Marrs, and Josh Mathews. Your friendship means the world to me.

The editorial team at B&H Academic® has been fantastic, improving my writing immensely through their deft editing. Logan Pyron and Renée Chavez deserve my thanks. Any errors in the book are mine alone and do not detract from Logan's and Renée's prowess with the pen.

I am grateful to congregations in New York City and suburban Portland for providing me the space to "practice what I preach," quite literally. Preaching on the frontier of unbelief in both cities has been a joyful adventure.

GENERAL INDEX

C